T0003838

AI AND WRITING

AI

AND WRITING

Sidney I. Dobrin

broadview press

BROADVIEW PRESS – www.broadviewpress.com
Peterborough, Ontario, Canada

Founded in 1985, Broadview Press remains a wholly independent publishing house. Broadview's focus is on academic publishing; our titles are accessible to university and college students as well as scholars and general readers. With over 800 titles in print, Broadview has become a leading international publisher in the humanities, with world-wide distribution. Broadview is committed to environmentally responsible publishing and fair business practices.

© 2023 Sidney I. Dobrin

All rights reserved. No part of this book may be reproduced, kept in an information storage and retrieval system, or transmitted in any form or by any means, electronic or mechanical, including photocopying, recording, or otherwise, except as expressly permitted by the applicable copyright laws or through written permission from the publisher.

Library and Archives Canada Cataloguing in Publication

Title: AI and writing / Sidney I. Dobrin.
Other titles: Artificial intelligence and writing
Names: Dobrin, Sidney I., 1967- author.
Description: Includes bibliographical references and index.
Identifiers: Canadiana (print) 20230505082 | Canadiana (ebook) 20230505139 | ISBN 9781554816514 (softcover) | ISBN 9781770489127 (PDF) | ISBN 9781460408445 (EPUB)
Subjects: LCSH: Authorship—Technological innovations. | LCSH: Writing—Automation. | LCSH: Artificial intelligence.
Classification: LCC PN171.T43 D63 2023 | DDC 808.00285/63—dc23

Broadview Press handles its own distribution in North America:
PO Box 1243, Peterborough, Ontario K9J 7H5, Canada
555 Riverwalk Parkway, Tonawanda, NY 14150, USA
Tel: (705) 743-8990; Fax: (705) 743-8353
email: customerservice@broadviewpress.com

For all territories outside of North America, distribution is handled by Eurospan Group.

Canadä Broadview Press acknowledges the financial support of the Government of Canada for our publishing activities.

Edited by Stephen Latta, Marjorie Mather, and Michel Pharand
Book Design by Em Dash Design

PRINTED IN CANADA

This one is in memory of my father,
Professor Leonard Dobrin.

CONTENTS

PREFACE

For the most part, formal writing instruction hasn't changed much over the last eighty years or so. And frankly, it hasn't needed to. The advent of "the writing process" provided writing instructors with replicable and teachable methods for showing students how to approach writing tasks systematically. The introduction of various modern technologies—the personal computer, word processors, and research tools such as Wikipedia—changed some of the details. But, in general, much of college-level writing instruction has remained focused on decades-old writing processes and centuries-old rhetorical approaches.

That changed on November 30, 2022, when OpenAI released ChatGPT to the public and teachers around the world faced a technology that some see as rendering the traditional writing process obsolete. ChatGPT, a Generative Artificial Intelligence (GenAI) chatbot that can produce seemingly original writing in just about any form requested, has disrupted higher education in ways never before seen. The velocity at which students began deploying ChatGPT caught writing instructors off guard. Most were ill-prepared to refine their long-standing instructional methods in light of a technology that can, in essence, bypass much of the traditional writing process.

AI and Writing is designed to help students and instructors understand how GenAI works and how to best integrate it within writing education. It's meant to function as a resource for writing-intensive courses, including courses in not only first-year writing but also advanced writing, professional writing, technical writing, and other specialized writing forms. It can be used independently as a primary textbook in a GenAI-focused course, or as an ancillary text used in conjunction with more traditional content. Its interdisciplinary approach makes *AI and Writing* particularly useful for "Writing Across the Curriculum" and "Writing in the Disciplines" programs.

This book provides practical instruction in how to use GenAI platforms to complete academic, professional, civic, and personal writing tasks. But it doesn't go so far as to teach the technical elements of specific platforms. This is because GenAI platforms are emerging and evolving so rapidly that to formalize such instruction in a textbook would inevitably make that book obsolete before the proverbial ink dried on the page. Instead, *AI and Writing* focuses on transferable skills that can assist student writers in many contexts and on many platforms. This advice is offered with the proviso that it should be implemented within the confines of an instructor's or institution's policies for GenAI use. In addition to this pragmatic instruction, *AI and Writing* takes up conceptual questions about the role of GenAI in the production of writing, as well as ethical questions about the use and development of GenAI.

APPARATUS

To achieve these goals, *AI and Writing* provides detailed and consistent apparatus throughout its ten chapters, including

- ▷ Learning Objectives for each chapter
- ▷ Before You Read This Chapter prompts, to encourage students to reflect on their preconceived ideas about the subject of each chapter
- ▷ Core content about each chapter's subject, presented in concise, accessible prose
- ▷ Provocations to encourage students to consider more complex conundrums related to GenAI and college-level writing
- ▷ "So What?" questions to push students to think about the relevance of GenAI
- ▷ Conceptual AI questions that ask students to engage with theoretical questions about GenAI and writing
- ▷ Applied AI questions that help students become familiar with the use of GenAI platforms, including their strengths and limitations
- ▷ Discussion Questions to encourage dialogue and the sharing of ideas about GenAI

In all, the apparatus of *AI and Writing* is designed to demystify GenAI for students and to help them understand how to deploy GenAI in a variety of writing forms.

AI AND WRITING AND GENERATIVE AI

As I emphasize throughout this book, transparency and documentation are paramount whenever GenAI is deployed. You may be curious, then, as to how much of this book was itself created by GenAI. The short answer is: not much. However, in several cases, I prompted GenAI platforms to identify key information and generate ideas. It was also used to confirm the usefulness of information arising out of my research and my own thinking. But none of the text in *AI and Writing* is wholesale copied from GenAI outputs (except where such outputs are quoted and properly cited as examples).

ACKNOWLEDGEMENTS

Though I've been working with emerging and evolving technologies in relation to writing and writing instruction for much of my career, by no means did *AI and Writing* unfold independently. Ongoing conversations and collaborations with the following colleagues have been indispensable to this book's authorship, and I am deeply grateful for their insights:

Raul Sanchez, University of Florida
Jason Crider, Texas A&M University
Sean Morey, University of Tennessee
Cath Ellis, University of New South Wales
Justin Hodgson, Indiana University Bloomington
Bill Hart-Davidson, Michigan State University
Todd Taylor, Adobe
Sebastian Distefano, Adobe
Manuela Franceschini, Adobe
Anton Rainer-Smith, Adobe
Sherman Young, RMIT University

I'm also grateful for all of the comments and questions from colleagues and students who've attended the talks, roundtables, task forces, and workshops about GenAI in which I've participated over the last eight months. Your questions and insights were invaluable.

I'm particularly grateful for the editorial input and encouragement of Marjorie Mather, Stephen Latta, and Dave Caulfield of Broadview Press, who not only made this project possible but who tolerated my chaotic and fast-paced approach to generating content. I'm grateful for this opportunity.

Of course, I'm also grateful for my many engagements with the various GenAI platforms, which not only inspired much of this book but also gave me pause to consider the very idea of the writing subject and of the value of writing instruction in higher education. Though I hate to quote Mark Zuckerberg, it is, indeed, time to move fast and break things.

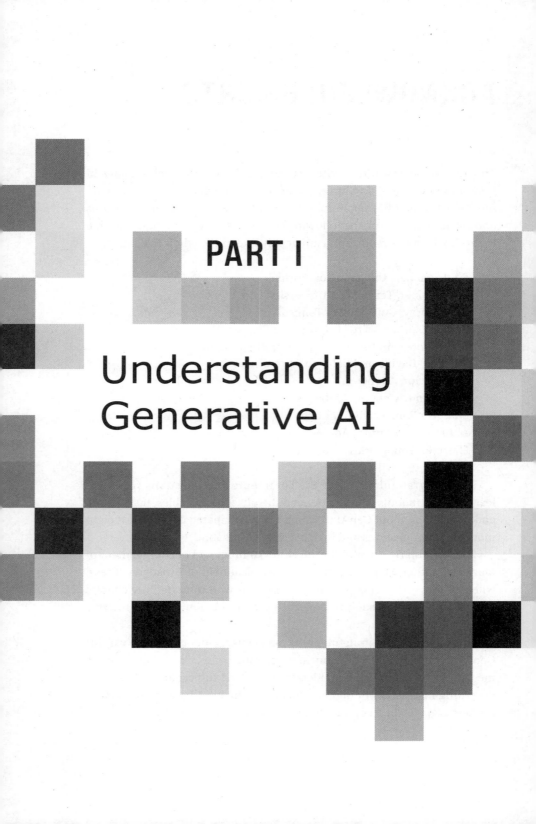

PART I

Understanding Generative AI

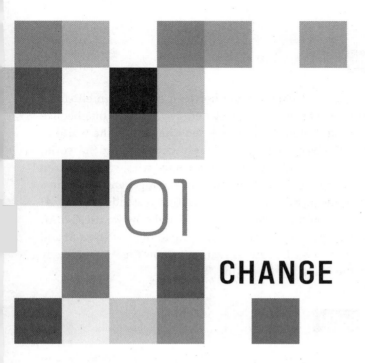

CHANGE

01

■ **LEARNING OBJECTIVES** ■

▷ Explain how new technologies can change a community.
▷ Recognize that generative writing technologies are not as new as many of us think.
▷ Analyze the histories of writing technologies and the cultural panic many of them caused.
▷ Differentiate between Conceptual AI and Applied AI.
▷ Examine the idea of human–machine collaboration in writing.
▷ Formulate methods for questioning the positive and negative aspects of GenAI technologies.

■ **BEFORE YOU READ THIS CHAPTER** ■

This book is about Artificial Intelligence and writing. Before you begin exploring this relationship, ask yourself: what do you understand "Artificial Intelligence" to mean? How does it work? Likewise, ask yourself what you understand about writing, what you learned about writing in elementary school and high school, and why it's studied and assigned in college. Think about your preconceived understandings about Artificial Intelligence and writing before you explore them in depth through this book.

INTRODUCTION

AI and Writing is about the interaction between Artificial Intelligence (AI)—including the new technologies of Generative Artificial Intelligence (GenAI)—and writing. When OpenAI released ChatGPT to the world in November 2022, high schools, colleges, and universities around the world, as well as just about every industry, were confronted with what appeared to be a dramatic change. This book is about that change, and about how we can engage with the possible challenges that GenAI stands to bring. *AI and Writing* is about how we understand GenAI and how we use GenAI. The next chapter will provide more detailed explanations as to how AI and GenAI work, but for now, we'll begin by examining how GenAI has already begun to change the landscape of writing.

INTRODUCING GenAI

Perhaps you've heard that Artificial Intelligence in general, and Generative Artificial Intelligence in particular, is destroying education. Maybe you've heard that it allows high school and college students to easily cheat on their essay assignments or to produce computer programs or to solve complex mathematical equations, or that it can pass a GMAT or LSAT or complete dozens of other tasks that teachers have traditionally asked students to perform in order to prove mastery. Perhaps you've seen the calls for colleges and universities to find ways to ban students from using GenAI applications such as OpenAI's ChatGPT (Chat Generative Pre-trained Transformer), Jasper, Hugging Face, and MidJourney.

Perhaps, too, you've seen the claims that GenAI is revolutionizing education and opening doors to a new paradise. Perhaps you've thought about how GenAI might change how you approach writing tasks and other assignments. Perhaps you've even used ChatGPT for this purpose already.

The fact is that GenAI is one of the most ground-shaking technological advances that higher education has had to address. Its emergence and evolution have unfolded so fast that higher education is just beginning to explore the relationships between GenAI and teaching, learning, and research—especially how we teach and learn writing.

Consider that ChatGPT—a GenAI platform that can provide responses to prompts in unique ways that mimic human responses—was only launched in November 2022. Within five days, over one million users logged on to ChatGPT. No other application has achieved that size of user base in that short of a time. The next fastest application was Instagram, the popular social media platform, which in 2010 took two and a half months to reach a million users. This kind of rapid adoption is unprecedented in digital applications. And a significant portion of these ChatGPT users are students.

ChatGPT's breakneck surge in popularity has exceeded that of any other computer application. While it took Instagram two and a half years to reach 100 million users, ChatGPT reached that level within two months of its public availability.

TIME TO 1 MILLION USERS[1]

ChatGPT	5 days
Spotify	5 months
Facebook	10 months
Twitter	2 years
Netflix	3.5 years

TIME TO 100 MILLION USERS[2]

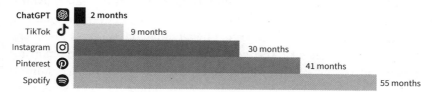

ChatGPT	2 months
TikTok	9 months
Instagram	30 months
Pinterest	41 months
Spotify	55 months

As the barrage of media coverage about GenAI and higher education illustrates, colleges and universities are trying to come to terms with how to address GenAI in the classroom, and writing intensive courses seem to be a primary site for understanding GenAI and education. While a handful of institutions have begun writing and posting policies for students using GenAI platforms, most have not, and many acknowledge that they are not yet prepared to engage teachers and students about GenAI. In a revealing survey published by *Best Colleges*, over half the college students surveyed in March of 2023 claimed that their instructors had not spoken with them about GenAI tools like ChatGPT.[3] Yet, in the same survey, 6 in 10 college students reported that their instructors or schools hadn't specified how to use AI tools ethically or responsibly.

Tellingly, 61 per cent of the students surveyed believed that GenAI will become part of everyday higher education and the way they work.

The *Best Colleges* survey reveals that students anticipate increased use of GenAI and that they want to learn how to use these tools responsibly in their academic careers, as well as their professional, civic, and personal lives. Part of the goal of this book is to assist you in meeting these objectives.

AUTOMATED WRITING: IT'S NOT REALLY NEW

In December 2013, the *Los Angeles Times* published a short article reporting that

> A shallow magnitude 4.7 earthquake was reported Monday morning 31 miles from Lone Pine, Calif., according to the U.S. Geological Survey. The temblor occurred at 5:39 a.m. PST near the surface....[4]

Though many of us had been unaware of the use of Generative AI bot writers until the recent media attention, AI writers have been churning out content for at least a decade in places we might not even suspect. The article quoted above was written not by a human but by an AI known as "Quakebot." Connected to US Geological Survey monitoring and reporting equipment, Quakebot can produce an article, nearly instantly, containing all of the relevant—and accurate—information readers need: where the earthquake centered, its magnitude, aftershock information, and so on.

AI writers are far more ubiquitous than most of us recognize. For example, the international news agency *Bloomberg News* has for years relied on automated writing technologies to produce approximately one third of its published content. *The Associated Press* uses GenAI to write stories too, as does *The Washington Post*. *Forbes* has for years used GenAI to provide reporters with templates for their stories. Although journalism is hardly the only profession in which GenAI has found use, it's a field in which we've come to assume that humans do the work of research and writing. Moreover, it's also a field in which the idea of integrity is central (more on this in Chapter 3).

Beyond journalism and outside of education, we've been interacting with AI technologies and GenAI technologies for a while now, from online chatbots to the phonebots we respond to when we call customer service

lines. Even many of the bulk emails we read are generated by GenAI platforms. AI-generated content has become omnipresent in our lives. And
more often than not, we remain ignorant as to whether the content we
read, hear, or see was produced by a writer or by a bot.

HISTORY OF WRITING TECHNOLOGIES AND CULTURAL PANIC

When ChatGPT brought the conversation about GenAI and education to
the public, much of the media coverage focused on concerns that this new
tool would launch a level of academic dishonesty never witnessed before,
as students would use GenAI to cheat on their assignments and circumvent their own learning. Education, particularly writing instruction, was
headed for crisis—if not total annihilation—at the hands of GenAI, many
media outlets proclaimed.

When it comes to technology, there's nothing new about the cries of
moral crisis. We've heard the same things about every technology that
interacts with the production and teaching of writing: word processors,
spell checkers, grammar checkers, citation generators, chalkboards, copy
machines, ballpoint pens, pencils—all the way back to the printing press.
In fact, there were fears of moral crisis that accompanied the introduction
of writing itself, which we sometimes forget is a technology, though an
ancient one.

In the early 2000s, when Wikipedia was launched, popular media was
filled with stories about students using it as their sole source rather than
conducting "actual research." Teachers and educational institutions held
meetings and filled syllabi with rules banning students from accessing
Wikipedia. Within a decade of Wikipedia's introduction, however, the educational outrage had dissipated, and many teachers now ask students to
write wiki pages or to revise and edit existing pages as commonplace writing assignments. They encourage students to go to Wikipedia to review articles in order to initiate their own research. They encourage them to read
Wikipedia pages as a way of generating ideas for their work. Since the initial
panic, Wikipedia has become a ubiquitous part of college education. In fact,
I recently saw Wikipedia identified as "an educational tool."

All technologies—not just digital technologies or writing technologies,
but *all* technologies—take two paths: either they become ubiquitous and
naturalized into the background of how we do things, or they become
obsolete. Sometimes they take both paths. In most cases, they become

obsolete because another technology has surpassed the old technology's usefulness or efficiency. In others, they become ubiquitous because they serve the needed purpose well enough—at least for the time being. No one picks up a spoon and marvels at it as a magnificent piece of technology. It is a ubiquitous technology, but it is a technology that drastically changed human culture. It altered social dynamics. It altered public health. It affected art and aesthetics. It impacted labor practices. It encouraged other technological developments. Technologically speaking, spoons and writing are quite similar. They are ancient technologies that have become ubiquitous, and are rarely thought of as technologies. Though writing has had far greater impacts on human history than spoons—and no doubt caused many more deaths—both have been integrated so thoroughly into our lives that we can easily forget that they are, in fact, technologies.

Media theorist Gregory Ulmer explains that when human culture evolved from the oral to the literate, the fundamental aspects of everything about humans and cultures changed (some for better, some for worse). The same thing is unfolding now as we move from a literate culture—a culture based in print reading, writing, and communication—to a post-literate culture or a digitally literate culture (what Ulmer terms "electracy"). Like the shifts from oral culture to literate culture, the shift to digital culture will change many aspects of who we are as human beings. These are big techno-philosophic developments, and they help us understand some of the worries regarding GenAI, for example that education won't be the same as it was for our parents and teachers. People worry that our accepted means of teaching, learning, and achieving success will be dramatically changed in ways that are challenging to imagine. GenAI may seem risky to education because it forces us to rethink the processes in which we are comfortably entrenched; it asks us—rather abruptly, it might seem—to change. Generative AI may not be destroying writing, however it may instead be reinvigorating it in new contexts. Either way, it requires us to think about some of the fundamental values and practices on which we've come to rely.

That doesn't mean we have to abandon everything we know about education or writing, or about what it means to learn. It means we have to integrate the old and the new. It means we have to apply some of our tried-and-true approaches to these new contexts, and we may have to change or even abandon some of our old ways of working and learning—just as the printing press, chalkboards, ballpoint pens, word processors, calculators, and even Wikipedia led to other changes and innovations.

Prior to November 2022, AI was only minimally a part of the academic landscape, with just a handful of academics (mostly in computer science disciplines) addressing the possibilities of GenAI's effect on higher education. When OpenAI made ChatGPT available to the public, mainstream media initiated a superficially critical storm about GenAI (with ChatGPT standing as a kind of generic branding for all GenAI). Fortunately, within a few weeks of the initial storm, the conversations shifted, in part, to more responsible questions about how educators might not just anticipate but also engage with GenAI in the classroom. Higher education began to take up what had become a six hundred pound trumpeting pink elephant in the classroom.

ChatGPT, of course, isn't the first technology to alarm writing instructors. However, the ChatGPT moment is fundamentally different for several reasons. First, it's not often that mainstream media picks up a story about higher education to the degree it covered—and continues to cover—ChatGPT's impact on education. That coverage brought the matter to the attention not just of educators but to a broader public audience, many of whom are invested in and care about education and make their thoughts known to higher education stakeholders.

Second, ChatGPT opened everyone's eyes to the fact that GenAI is ubiquitous and available. This is not a hard-to-get, hard-to-use, specialized piece of technology. Likewise, given the possibilities of broad-scope use, from writing essays for English classes to writing computer codes for computer sciences classes, and even to taking GMATs or LSATs, ChatGPT brought to the fore the fact that GenAI is not limited to only a small number of select disciplines. For many academics, the very fact that they themselves could open and use ChatGPT easily and without any technical training moved GenAI from being a thing about which they were at most vaguely aware to something that had the potential to be used widely. The ChatGPT media moment put GenAI directly in the laps of all teachers and students—whether they wanted it there or not.

The wake-up call of November 2022 should not, however, be seen as the alarm signaling the fall of higher education or the demise of teaching and learning, as some have suggested. Rather, the arrival of an accessible, public version of ChatGPT provides an opportunity to begin wider-ranging conversations about higher ed's long-term interaction with GenAI.

CONCEPTUAL AND APPLIED AI

In the next chapter, we'll look specifically at what *Artificial Intelligence* and *Generative Artificial Intelligence* mean and how they work. For now, you should understand that we familiarly—and reductively—define Artificial Intelligence as both the theory and development of computer systems that can perform tasks that previously required human intelligence.

This definition provides two key approaches to how we think about AI: the theoretical, or what we might call the conceptual, and the applicable. Thus, we can think about AI from both perspectives: Conceptual AI and Applied AI.

Conceptual AI is about the ramifications or consequences of AI. Conceptual AI asks questions about things like how AI might impact societies, economies, and cultures. It addresses AI's impacts on how we teach and learn writing. Conceptual AI also takes up the ethical issues that surround AI's evolution and use, and how we might further develop specific AI technologies. Conceptual AI addresses questions of *Why* and *What If*.

Applied AI, on the other hand, asks questions about how to *use* AI, both generally and specifically. It focuses on practicality and use, as well as the development of new AI applications. Applied AI focuses on questions of *How*.

Conceptual AI and Applied AI are two sides of a single coin, and both are necessary for understanding, making, and using AI technologies. To engage with AI responsibly, we all need to understand the hows, the what-ifs, and the whys of AI.

HUMAN–MACHINE COLLABORATION

One way we might think about deploying GenAI in our writing is to think of our interactions with GenAI as a kind of human–machine collaboration. Not all writing is done individually. In many contexts, we collaborate with others to create a single writing product. Some college assignments require teamwork, and much of professional writing is collaborative. There are usually two fundamental goals of collaboration. The first is to bring a range of experiences, expertise, and opinions to bear on a writing task. The second is to distribute the labor of a writing task equally among the members of the collaborative team. Each of these goals includes sub-objectives that can benefit the writers and the writing: reducing an individual's labor commitment, increasing attention to accuracy, and completing writing tasks quicker.

Collaborative writing can take many forms. For example:

▷ A lead author composes the primary draft and then collaborators revise it. This is a common approach in much scientific writing.

▷ Collaborators work sequentially, each adding their input and passing the document to the next collaborator.

▷ Collaborators each compose their individual segments of the overall project and then one or more of them compiles the segments into a single document.

▷ Each collaborator performs an assigned task based on individual expertise or agreed-upon labor distribution. For example, one group member might conduct the primary research, one might revise the draft, one might copyedit and proofread it, and one might typeset and design the final version.

▷ The entire group discusses, plans, drafts, edits, and revises the document together from the outset to completion.

Much of the public conversation about GenAI and writing has focused on using it to complete entire writing tasks from beginning to end, such as having a GenAI write an assigned essay about *Moby-Dick*. But this isn't the only option. GenAI also allows for human–machine collaboration, which involves the sharing of labor between the human writer and the AI writer.

Think of human–machine collaboration like this: in order for an automotive manufacturer to assemble a car, parts of the vehicle are put together by an automated system (robotics) and parts are put together by human workers. The quality of the assembly is checked by both human experts and by mechanical sensors. This form of machine-human collaboration takes the best parts of what the human and the machine can provide to create a superior product more efficiently.

When it comes to writing, we can think of GenAI and human collaboration in the same way: both the human and the AI provide expertise and labor in order to successfully complete the task at hand. The real value in human–machine collaboration is that it allows us to think of GenAI not only as a tool to complete a task but also as a potentially important way to augment our own writing abilities. Human–machine collaboration can free a writer from the mundane tasks of writing, allowing them to focus on ideas, critical thinking, and problem-solving.

Another way that human–machine collaboration can work is for you to "talk" with a GenAI platform about ideas in the same way you might talk with a classmate, a roommate, a friend, or a family member. GenAI chatbots can offer insights into your writing in ways that, in some cases, a writing tutor cannot.

Keep in mind that for now, GenAI platforms are limited in their abilities. The information they supply can be inaccurate or biased. They can produce repetitive text that is often flat and undynamic. They also require significant training. Ultimately, as with automotive manufacturing, the success of human–machine collaboration in writing requires significant human participation. GenAI may not be able to do your writing for you, but it may be able to function as a valuable collaborator.

Let's be honest about collaboration, too: we all want collaborators who are capable of offering novel contributions to our work. Think back to those moments in high school when you had to choose a lab partner, and how students rushed to pair with the "smart kid" hoping their own grade would benefit from that student's work. In many ways, GenAI can be that smart kid for all of us.

Provocation

If GenAI can produce writing that is good enough in some contexts, can help you more efficiently and effectively respond to writing assignments, can complete many mundane aspects of writing tasks like citation formatting or grammar checking, do we need to continue to teach writing in high schools, colleges, and universities? Should college students be required to take first-year writing, as they have for decades? Has GenAI rendered composition classes obsolete, or in need of a curricular overhaul?

SO WHAT?

One of the most important questions we can ask about just about anything is "So what?" Not in a dismissive way, as we might offhandedly say when we don't care about something. "The cardboard box is brown. So? So what? Who cares?"—but in a more critical, rigorous, inquisitive way:

▷ "GenAI can help to write an essay on *Moby-Dick* ... so what does that mean to me?"

▷ "Most college writing curricula don't integrate GenAI at present ... so what does that tell us?"

▷ "Many plagiarism policies were developed prior to the existence of GenAI ... so what does that mean in terms of how we should or shouldn't use GenAI?"

One of the underlying questions that drives this book is "So what?" This book is designed to encourage you to ask the *so what* questions about GenAI and writing. Throughout, you'll find many *so what* moments, and at the end of each chapter, you'll find a set of *so what* questions, designed to elicit reflective responses about the implications of these new technologies.

USERS AREN'T LOSERS

GenAI is often talked about in popular media as, at best, an uncomfortable topic: "Have you talked with your kid about drinking and driving? About drugs? About GenAI?" The alarmist messaging echoes anti-drug campaigns: "Don't do GenAI." "Users are Losers." "Just say no to GenAI." "Choose not to use."

Of course I'm being hyperbolic. Yet, just as with drugs, avoiding discussion of GenAI as an academic tool can leave students curious about what it is, what it does, and how to use it responsibly. Those curiosities are normal—and should be encouraged. While many colleges and universities are working to establish formal policies toward GenAI, many are not, and many acknowledge that they are not yet prepared to offer directions to either instructors or students regarding the responsible use of GenAI.

Not talking about AI and GenAI can make the subject seem sinister: "We're not going to talk about that" [avoids eye contact]. It may even make you want to try it privately—back-alley GenAI. At a recent conference, I asked a group of students, "How many of you have tried ChatGPT?" It wasn't so much the numbers of students that raised their hands that was telling, but rather the numbers who looked around the room first trying to decide if it was ok to admit they had used GenAI. I might as well have asked, "How many of you cheated on an important assignment?" or "How many of you had a beer before you were of legal age?" None wanted to admit they'd used GenAI until they were certain they weren't alone.

The idea that using GenAI is a form of academic dishonesty is prevalent in discussions about GenAI and higher education. In the *Best Colleges* survey discussed earlier, 51 per cent of students said they believe using GenAI technologies is a form of plagiarism, though about 20 per cent said they use these tools anyway.[5] Yet there is much uncertainty about the application of current plagiarism policies to GenAI, and it may be that we need to revisit how we understand academic integrity (more on this in Chapter 3).

In the pages that follow, you'll find explanations of how GenAI works. You'll also find many questions about how it might be used, and about the ramifications of using it. These questions are designed to encourage exploration. No matter what you think the value of AI is, the general consensus is that these technologies will become ubiquitous parts of our lives, and will change the way we do and think about things. The emerging and evolving technologies of AI extend well beyond the purview or expertise of any one discipline. In fact, some experts have gone so far as to say that AI will change the course of human history. *AI and Writing* is designed with a more limited goal in mind: to help you think about how GenAI is likely to change writing and the way you write.

END OF CHAPTER MATERIALS

So What?

1. As discussed in this chapter, GenAI may play (or come to play) an important role in writing. So what? Why should we talk about GenAI in the context of college writing in particular?

2. GenAI raises many issues with regard to responsible writing. So what? Which of these issues do you think is most important?

Conceptual AI

1. For many of us, how we think about AI is informed by media represen-
    tations. We're particularly influenced by fictional representations in
    film, comics, books, and other media. Many of these representations
    are characterized as science fiction, or what is often called "specula-
    tive fiction." In what ways have such representations informed how
    you think about AI? What media representations of AI stand out for
    you? How do you think those media representations inform how we
    are responding to GenAI's role in college education?

2. In what ways do you see GenAI affecting how we teach and learn writ-
    ing in college, both positively and negatively?

3. We rely significantly on all kinds of technologies in our lives, includ-
    ing some that we don't often think of as technologies: we wear textile
    technologies (clothes); we wear ocular correcting technologies (eye-
    glasses and contact lenses); we rely on pharmaceutical technologies
    (vaccinations and medicines); we depend on transportation technol-
    ogies (airplanes and automobiles); we count on agricultural technolo-
    gies (pesticides and harvest equipment); we count on communications
    technologies (mobile devices and the internet); and so on. Given our
    dependence upon technologies, why do you suppose AI as an emerg-
    ing and evolving technology is both embraced and contested? Write
    a short paper outlining why and how you think AI is or isn't different
    from other technologies we depend upon.

Applied AI

1. One of the more popular ways of learning more about what GenAI can
    and cannot do is to have a discussion with a GenAI chatbot—such as
    ChatGPT—about what it does. Using a GenAI platform, have a discus-
    sion with the bot to determine what it does and does not do.

2. As more and more GenAI platforms become available, they each pro-
    vide different kinds of expertise and different capabilities. Locate five
    GenAI platforms that are specifically designed to provide written out-
    put in response to prompts. Identify their differences. Which ones are
    best for student use?

3. In order to get a sense of how GenAI platforms write, try this:

   a. Select a historical figure, someone you admire or are interested in learning more about. This should be someone well-known, so that a GenAI can locate information about them.
   b. Ask a GenAI application (like ChatGPT) to write a biographical essay about that figure.
   c. Next, using the same GenAI platform, prompt the GenAI to write lyrics for a song in the style of one of your favorite artists about the same historical figure it has produced the essay about. For example, write a rap song in the style of Wu-Tang Clan about Julius Caesar; or write a song in the style of Taylor Swift about Leonardo da Vinci; or write a song in the style of CHAI about Cleopatra.
   d. Compare the song lyrics with the essay about that person. What stands out to you in this comparison?

For Discussion

1. Have you used GenAI? If so, in what capacity? What were your experiences?

2. Given the overview provided in this chapter, what are your thoughts about how GenAI will impact or change your college writing experiences?

02

GENERATIVE AI

▦ LEARNING OBJECTIVES ▦

▷ Describe the evolution of Artificial Intelligence.
▷ Discuss the development of Generative Artificial Intelligence.
▷ Explain the basic operations of Generative Artificial Intelligence.
▷ Identify ways in which Generative Artificial Intelligence challenges higher education, especially writing instruction.
▷ Recognize the problem of hallucinations.

▦ BEFORE YOU READ THIS CHAPTER ▦

Popular media, news media, and social media have been inundated with articles and stories about GenAI and its effect on the world, and especially its impact on education. But how and why did we develop the idea and the technologies of AI and GenAI in the first place? This chapter provides an overview of those histories as well as an introduction to how GenAI works. Before reading the chapter, consider what you already know about AI and GenAI and how those concepts and technologies evolved and became important to education.

INTRODUCTION

Most college teachers and administrators were caught off guard by the sudden public emergence of GenAI and are still unsure how best to respond to it. Part of the confusion grew from a general lack of awareness as to what AI or GenAI actually is. For most people, AI evokes images of movies and television, not classroom writing. This chapter provides a brief overview of the history of AI development in order to demystify what AI and GenAI actually do and how they do it.

AI'S ORIGINS

AI and GenAI technologies are not as new as many think, and neither are the core ideas from which AI technologies grow. In fact, throughout history, humans have imagined ways of imbuing non-human objects with varying degrees of intelligence in order to assist with various tasks. Here are a few examples:

> ▷ In the *Iliad,* written more than three thousand years ago, Homer tells stories of Hephaestus the Greek god of fire, metalwork, stonemasonry, and craftsmanship. Hephaestus crafted golden robot-like statues that served him and were able to speak and offer their thoughts. He also built two immortal mechanical dogs to guard the palace of Alcinous, and mechanical tables that would serve the gods food and drink when ordered to do so.

> ▷ The collection of Middle Eastern folk tales commonly known in the West as *One Thousand and One Arabian Nights,* which compiles stories that date between the eighth and thirteenth centuries, includes "The Story of the City of Brass." In this story, a band of travelers encounter a mechanical brass horseman who offers travelers directions for safe passage on the road.

> ▷ The Jewish legend of the Golem tells the story of lifeless substances like dirt or clay shaped into the form of a person and brought to life by a human creator to serve as a companion, a helper, and a protector who could rescue a Jewish community from peril.

> ▷ In the eighteenth and nineteeth centuries, the idea of mechanical assistants was popular in fiction. In E.T.A. Hoffmann's story "Der

Sandmann" ("The Sandman"), the protagonist falls in love with a woman only to learn that she is a machine. When he realizes he is in love with an automaton, he chooses to die by suicide.

▷ One year after Hoffmann published "The Sandman," Mary Shelley published *Frankenstein; or, The Modern Prometheus* (1818), in which Dr. Victor Frankenstein gives sentience to a non-living creature.

▷ The word 'robot' was coined in a 1920 play by Czech playwright Karel Čapek titled *R.U.R.*, which stands for *Rossum's Universal Robots*. The play, arguably the first instance of the fictional theme of robot uprising, tells the story of mechanical figures used to perform menial labor who grow weary of being exploited and rise up to kill their human masters. "Robot" is taken from the Old Slavonic word *robata*, which means "forced labor." According to AI scholar Kanta Dihal, "The robot revolt in R.U.R. parallels the labour revolts of the nineteenth and early twentieth centuries, but also recalls both abolitionist and anti-abolitionist discourse in its focus on the economic benefits these wageless new creations bring."[6]

While ideas about Artificial Intelligence can be traced to many human histories and cultures, the emergence and evolution of AI as we understand it really began in 1943 when John Mauchly and J. Presper Eckert, at the Moore School of Electrical Engineering of the University of Pennsylvania, developed the first general purpose, electronic, and programmable computer. Known as the ENIAC Computing System, this computer weighed over thirty tons, used eighteen thousand vacuum tubes (the larger and bulkier predecessor to the modern transistor), and took up a thousand square feet of space. Because it was electric rather than electromechanical, it could compute at a rate one thousand times faster than any previous computational machine. ENIAC was capable of performing about 385 multiplication operations per second. Consider that the iPhone 14 (released in September 2022, two months before ChatGPT) can perform approximately 15.8 trillion operations per second—that's almost 42 billion times the computing power of ENIAC.

What ENIAC triggered was a different form of inquiry about what machines could do. The introduction of ENIAC inspired people to ask questions about whether or not machines could think, whether they could think like humans, and whether they could be intelligent.

Seven years after the development of ENIAC, mathematician and computer scientist Alan Turing attempted to answer these questions in his

ENIAC

article "Computing Machinery and Intelligence."[7] Turing suggested that trying to figure out if a machine was intelligent was not what mattered; what mattered was the machine's ability to perform or display intelligence. Turing argued that since we can never know how other beings think, we cannot really judge their intelligence; however, we can judge whether their behavior displays intelligence. Unfortunately, Turing didn't take up the philosophical question as to what "intelligence" is, a quandary that still plagues our thinking about AI. However, he did propose what he called the "Imitation Game," which would evolve to be known as the Turing Test. The object of the Turing Test is to see if a machine can do things like answer questions or play games such that a human could not tell whether these actions were performed by a human or a machine. The Turing Test posited that if a machine could imitate human response to the degree that a human could not tell they were interacting with a machine, then the machine displayed or performed intelligence.

In 1956, computer scientist John McCarthy, one of the founders of Artificial Intelligence as an academic discipline, first co-coined the term *Artificial Intelligence* in a document he co-authored proposing a conference about the subject. McCarthy defined AI as "the science and engineering of making intelligent machines," and he extended Turing's notion of machines performing intelligence by holding that AI machines are those "that can perform tasks that are characteristic of human intelligence." The combination of Turing's and McCarthy's definitions resulted in our common understanding of AI not as actual intelligence but as the *performance* of what appears to be intelligent behavior.

Early attempts to build AI focused on compiling fact-based rule sets. However, many of these attempts were not very effective because, in human thinking, rules are often mutable and contextual rather than concrete and universal. Thus, early attempts to build AI were most successful in fields that employ stringent rule-based knowledge, like mathematics or system automation. However, in areas that are substantially more contextual—such as voice recognition, language translation, or image recognition—early AI systems could not adapt appropriately. Their inflexible, rule-driven approaches to "thinking" made them too rigid for these purposes.

For example, imagine trying to design an AI to identify fish in pictures. There are over 33,000 species of fish, and it is estimated that there are more than 3.5 trillion individual fish in the world. While we, as human thinkers, might be able to identify a picture of a fish no matter how different the fish look from one another, early AI rule-based programming could not. Consider these three pictures (yes, they are all photographs of real fish):

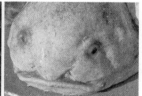

A rule-driven AI might look for consistent characteristics such as fins, gills, and tails. But identifying a fin on each of these fish might be difficult. Likewise, because fish move and turn and flex or retract their fins, pictures of fish are inconsistent in what they represent. It's also likely that many people only recognize the angler fish (left) as a fish because images of this species have been popularized in familiar media like the *Finding Nemo* movie. The blobfish (right) became familiar to some of us in 2013 when it earned the moniker "world's ugliest animal" and appeared in news media as a result. The trout (center) is common to rivers and lakes across the US and clearly exhibits familiar characteristics like tails, fins, and gills. These variations make it virtually impossible for early rule-based AI programs to determine whether an image shows a fish.

This problem of contextual thinking was difficult for AI developers to overcome, and for a long time AI development stagnated. In 1984, some researchers claimed that we had entered an "AI Winter," a time when interest in and funding for AI development withered. Within a few years AI research and development began to collapse, as general pessimism about the future of AI led to the loss of billions of dollars in funding.

However, in the 1990s, a few remaining AI researchers shifted tactics. Rather than programming AI with rule-based data on which to base decisions, they hypothesized that AIs could be programmed with learning processes. That is, the machines could be taught to learn.

THE NEW AI

As we begin to discuss contemporary AI and GenAI, it is important to understand the differences between traditional computer programs and machine learning.

Traditional computer programs are, in essence, sets of linear instructions delivered to the computer. For example, one of the first programming strings coders using Basic are taught is the If/Then structure. It is a basic formula that simply conveys "if this, then that." It's a straightforward, linear set of instructions that looks something like this:

001 If A = 10 then goto 025

002 If A < 10 then goto 026

003 if A > 10 then goto 027

Machine learning—the process used in developing modern AI—does not operate in this kind of linear fashion. Instead, AI uses specific algorithms—processes or sets of rules or instructions used for solving problems—that "learn" from each engagement and then make predictions and decisions as to what the next action might be based on previous experiences in performing similar tasks. This is known as *machine learning*. Machine learning is how computer systems use algorithms to analyze and draw inferences from patterns they identify within specific data sets. When an AI recognizes patterns within a data set, it "learns" to make inferences about those patterns. In this way, machine learning requires

AI systems to "train" using predetermined data sets in order for the AI to "learn" to identify patterns in those sets. Reductively, then, machine learning comprises the ways in which a computer learns from the data it encounters in order to perform tasks without being programmed specifically to perform those tasks. That is, modern AI adjusts based upon what it learns rather than adhering to a set of pre-programmed rules. Machine learning is a central component of GenAI.

In addition to machine learning, AI algorithms can also use deep learning techniques for processing information. Deep learning can be thought of as a series of complex algorithms that are modeled on the human brain and the structures humans use to think. This allows the AI to work with unlike and unstructured data such as images, alphabetic text, sound, and so on. Machine learning and deep learning allow an AI to adjust to contexts and to feedback in order to provide adaptive responses to new tasks.

This recent period of AI development also saw the return to an early idea that Frank Rosenblatt of the Cornell Aeronautical Laboratory introduced in 1958: that a computer could be programmed to take in and process information in the same way as a human brain. This is now known as a **neural network**. A neural network is a mathematical system that scans large amounts of data to identify patterns. The AI processes the data in those patterns to "learn" the characteristics of the data. For example, an AI might classify a recurring pattern identifying that *Moby-Dick* was a novel written by Herman Melville in 1851. It might also discern from those patterns that *Moby-Dick* is the title of the book and Moby Dick is the name of the whale in the book. It can only do so, however, if there are multiple statements that identify this information so as to create a pattern. Similarly, a neural network can look for patterns in images of, say for example, a whale in order to identify what a whale is. This is also how voice recognition AI is able to "understand" what you mean when you say "pay bill" in response to an automated customer service prompt. This process of scouring large data sets and learning from them is how machine learning and deep learning function and how contemporary AI operates.

GENERATIVE ARTIFICIAL INTELLIGENCE

In 2014, Ian Goodfellow, a computer scientist known for his work with deep learning and AI neural networks, along with his colleagues, proposed a new approach to machine learning called Generative Adversarial Networks

(GANs). This new type of machine learning algorithm allowed AIs to generate what appears to be original output. For example, using GANs, an AI can analyze patterns found in pictures of fish and then generate a new image of what it predicts a fish to look like. GANs operate by using a neural network to locate patterns within a data set and then generating a new output that fits within those patterns. This part of the GANs operation is known as the generator. What makes GANs so effective is that they use a second neural network, called a discriminator, which indirectly checks how realistic the generator's output is and trains the AI to account for that proximity so as to improve its accuracy in future tasks. GANs make it possible for AIs to generate what appears to be original content, including convincingly authentic images, videos, audio, formulas, computer code, writing, and much more.

By 2018, several AI-focused companies, including Google and Microsoft, began building and using neural networks that could scour and scrape massive amounts of complex data from the internet. These new neural networks could access data from Wikipedia, digitized books, academic publications, and anything else publicly available on the internet. These extensive data sets are known as **Large Language Models** (LLM). By identifying patterns within LLMs and then reorganizing the information in those patterns, GANs-driven AI machines were able to produce writing or images that appear original and that resemble the work of human creators. This is Generative Artificial Intelligence.

Essentially, then, GenAI is a class of AI algorithms that can generate a variety of content—including text, images, and sounds—based on patterns it has identified within a data set.

As it evolves, the kinds of outputs that GenAI can produce expands, and the accuracy and efficiency of its outputs improves, particularly as users train GenAI platforms to produce outputs that fit specific needs. While *AI and Writing* focuses primarily on writing, GenAI is being used for so much more: image generation, image revision, medical imaging, video production, 3D modeling, text-to-speech, language translation, music generation, sentiment analysis, code generation, code analysis, code debugging, code proofing, material design, data synthesis, data analysis, curriculum development, teaching and tutoring, game design, game generation, character behavior, facial recognition, identity verification, customer service, consumer reviews, rapid responses to inquiries, email generation, audience research, product descriptions, mathematical formulas—and so on!

HOW GENERATIVE AI WORKS

Because the ways in which GenAI is being used are growing rapidly, it's valuable to understand how GenAI works, even in a rudimentary way. In summary, GenAI works like this:

▷ A user provides the AI with a prompt asking the AI to generate a specific deliverable—an essay, a song, an image, the solution to a math problem, a computer program, and so on. (Of course, the AI system must be able to produce the kind of output in order to respond, so an AI that is not designed to generate images, for example, can't provide an image in response to a prompt requesting an image.)

▷ The AI then "scrubs" through all of the data available to it looking for patterns and recurring information about the requested task.

▷ It then reorganizes that data into a pattern that it deems to answer the prompt.

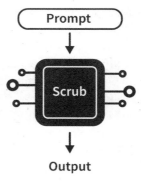

We can think of a GenAI as participating in a rudimentary conversation with a user. The user asks a question, the AI locates the information, and the AI answers the user's request. This is how chatbots function and why ChatGPT is called ChatGPT (Chat Generative Pre-trained Transformer): it is a complex chatbot that is pre-trained to locate data and transform that data in order to generate new ways of conveying that data.

In addition to responding based upon the "training" they receive within their LLM, GenAI platforms learn from each encounter they have with a user. How the user prompts the GenAI platform to perform a task helps the

GenAI learn new ways to approach a problem. That is, GenAI improves not just through its pre-training but also through each act it performs.

However, there are several problems with current iterations of GenAI. For example, currently AIs aren't able to discern value, accuracy, or bias in the data they scrub. They are only able to identify data and patterns within that data, and thus they often incorporate inaccurate, false, or biased information (see the section on hallucinations below). Nor can AIs identify which data are more or less relevant in light of a provided

Provocation

The concern about GenAI's access to only digitized data ties directly to the ways in which we learn about and employ research methodologies and critical assessments of research materials and data. However, these issues are not unique to GenAI. Over the past decade, several graduate and undergraduate students have told me that "if it's not online, it's not usable research." This emerging research atmosphere raises several issues about research and education that require further consideration, including the ways in which we account for non-digitized research availability, the function of non-digitized texts, and even our understanding as to what a campus library provides. This stance about research appears to be growing to a commonplace assumption among students. It leaves a tremendous amount of research outside the "useful" pool. It also brings to bear the distinctions we make about what counts as digitization, as simply scanning documents doesn't necessarily make them accessible if they cannot be scrubbed for individual terms, images, and such.

Introducing GenAI technologies entails that we must consider the availability of digital research in two key ways: 1) accessibility of research to the LLMs and 2) student understanding of what constitutes viable research in an age of digital access. From your perspective, what constitutes viable research? Do you rely only on information you can access digitally? Why or why not?

prompt. Thus, we must be critical when assessing the accuracy and the relevance of GenAI outputs.

Likewise, GenAI systems can only gather information from the LLMs to which they have access. Data that hasn't been digitized or is not available to the AI's access will never be part of what the AI can generate. This limit of access restricts what an AI can generate and, in turn, affects the value of the AI's output. This question of data access and limit will continue to be an important difficulty not only in educational contexts, but also for many research and development situations.

LLM data sets are always limited. They may be massive, but they have boundaries. And because GenAI neural networks look for patterns within an LLM and then generate outputs based on which patterns repeat most frequently, many GenAI applications reinscribe the same biased information they encounter, thus reinforcing the same old entrenched data and perspectives. See Chapter 9 for more information on the many ways in which LLM data sets and GenAI outputs can be biased.

HALLUCINATIONS

GenAIs are susceptible to returning what are known as **hallucinations:** outputs that are false despite appearing correct. Hallucinations can result from insufficient data, unclear prompting, limited data in an LLM, overly specialized data, or data bias. In writing, hallucinations may even include false quotes, fake sources, and fabricated data.

For example, I recently prompted ChatGPT-3 to write an academic biography for a grant I was proposing. Using the prompt "write an academic biography of Sidney I. Dobrin," ChatGPT-3 returned a 544-word essay, which, if you did not know me or my work, would sound as though it were correct. The information in the essay appears correct, but almost none of it is. A few examples:

> He pursued his academic journey by earning a Bachelor's degree in English and Linguistics from the University of Pittsburgh. Recognizing the importance of rhetoric in understanding the complexities of human communication, Dobrin went on to complete his Master's degree in Rhetoric and Communication at the same institution.[8]

This sounds like something I might have done, but I have never attended the University of Pittsburgh, never worked there, never even visited the campus. It's a great university, but I have no affiliation with it. I earned my BA from Virginia Wesleyan College (now University) in Virginia Beach and my Master's degree from Old Dominion University in Norfolk, VA. My Master's is in Rhetoric and Composition, not "Rhetoric and Communication."

> Dobrin's pursuit of knowledge and passion for teaching propelled him to further his education. He enrolled at the University of Texas at Austin, where he earned his Ph.D. in Rhetoric and Composition. During his doctoral studies, Dobrin immersed himself in the scholarship of composition pedagogy, rhetorical theory, and cultural studies. This multidisciplinary approach would become a hallmark of his academic career.

Nope. I earned my PhD from the University of South Florida, and my research focused on composition theories and pedagogies. It would be a stretch to say I immersed myself in rhetorical theory or cultural studies, but all of this sounds like it *could* be true.

> He held faculty positions at prestigious institutions such as the University of Florida, the University of Kansas, and the University of Texas at Austin.

Well, two of the three are right. I am faculty at the University of Florida and was faculty at the University of Kansas. But I have never worked at the University of Texas.

> His expertise and dedication to the discipline garnered recognition, leading him to serve as the Chair of the Conference on College Composition and Communication (CCCC) and as the President of the Association for Rhetoric of Science, Technology, and Medicine (ARSTM).

Nope. Not even close. Yes, I have been a member of CCCC, but never held the Chair position, and honestly, I've never heard of ARSTM.

> Dobrin's scholarly output is characterized by its breadth and depth. His research encompasses a diverse array of topics,

including the impact of digital technologies on writing and literacy, the relationship between rhetoric and environmental studies, and the intersection of rhetoric and social justice. His groundbreaking book, "Postcomposition," challenged conventional notions of writing and composition, exploring the ways in which digital media and multimodal communication have reshaped the landscape of writing instruction and practice.

This is mostly correct (that's not exactly what *Postcomposition* is, though it's close). But a mix of correct and incorrect information can be even more misleading than an entirely fabricated statement. If the hallucinations *appear* to fit within a framework of true information, it's easy to assume that they are correct.

This example is by no means an outlier. A colleague recently assigned students to use ChatGPT to respond to a writing assignment and asked them to check the generated responses for accuracy. Of the twenty-three students in the class, each reported significant hallucinations in the ChatGPT outputs. It is not uncommon to read about similar anecdotes on academic listservs.

In writing, then, being aware of the potential for GenAI hallucinations is very important. With GenAI visuals, the effect can be equally problematic and perhaps even more disconcerting. Consider this image generated by the GenAI program Dall-E when prompted with "hands playing on a piano":[9]

As you can see there's something not quite right about the left hand. This too is a hallucination.

Hallucinations are considered a significant problem for LLMs and GenAI. Imagine the impact a hallucination might have if a GenAI reported to investors that sales of a product had increased by ten per cent over the last quarter when sales had, in fact, dropped. If the GenAI used to produce the report did not have access to accurate data, it may have speculated based on information from earlier reports. Or suppose you were creating an academic essay about a novel using a GenAI program, and it simply fabricated certain key events, even using direct quotes. How might your instructor respond?

END OF CHAPTER MATERIALS

So What?

1. Suppose GenAI continues to evolve. So what? Given your assumptions, what might be the ramifications for your educational and professional careers?

2. GenAI hallucination is common and not always easy to identify. So what does this suggest about the reliability of using AI-generated material without oversight?

3. Is GenAI intelligent, according to the Turing Test? If it is, what does this mean with regard to our understanding of intelligence?

Conceptual AI

1. Throughout this chapter, there is an underlying question about whether or not a machine can think like a human or perform tasks like a human. Conceptually, why does it matter if the machine's operations work like a human's or display the characteristics of human thinking? What are the ramifications of such ideas on how we understand AI and how we understand humans and human thinking?

2. Why do you suppose humans have wanted to imbue non-human objects with "intelligence" in order to have those objects either

perform our work for us or make our work easier or more efficient? That is, what drives us to defer some of the things we do to machines?

3. Is "Artificial Intelligence" an accurate term? Is it the right term to use? Why or why not?

4. Suppose someone were to ask you, "what's the point of having Artificial Intelligence?" How would you respond? Write a short essay in which you explain your views on the value and/or dangers of AI and GenAI.

5. The Future of Life Institute (FLI) is an organization dedicated to "steering transformative technology towards benefiting life and away from extreme large-scale risks" and to reducing "large-scale harm, catastrophe, and existential risk resulting from accidental or intentional misuse of transformative technologies." In 2017, FLI hosted the Beneficial AI conference, which brought together "AI researchers from academia and industry, and thought leaders in economics, law, ethics, and philosophy for five days dedicated to beneficial AI."[10] During the conference, attendees collaboratively developed a series of twenty-three principles for developing AI. Named for the location of the conference, the Asilomar Principles have become some of the most important guidelines for AI development. Nearly 6,000 researchers, developers, industry leaders, and government officials have signed and endorsed these guidelines.

In March 2023, FLI published "Pause Giant AI Experiments: An Open Letter" calling for "all AI labs to immediately pause for at least 6 months the training of AI systems more powerful than GPT-4."[11] The letter has been signed by more than 31,000 technology development leaders, including Elon Musk, Steve Wozniak, Andrew Yang, Rachel Bronson, and Tristan Harris.

Take some time to read and consider both the FLI principles and the FLI moratorium letter (available on the FLI web pages). Then consider your response to both documents. With these two well-known documents in mind, write a response explaining your thoughts about the future of AI and GenAI development.

Applied AI

1. Most GenAI programs cannot deliver multiple, improved drafts of a piece of writing without specific additional prompts from a human user. In light of this, what might be some beneficial ways to use GenAI

in your writing, other than simply having a GenAI write the response on the whole?

2. Using a GenAI image platform of your choice, create pictures of a specific object or scenario, such as "college students," "kids at a basketball game," or "walking on a dirt road." What kinds of familiar returns do you get? Are there biases evident in the output?

3. Using ChatGPT (or any other GenAI platform that you have access to), generate a document that describes the evolution of contemporary GenAI technologies. Compare the GenAI's output with the information found in this chapter. Which do you find more useful? Which is more accurate? How do you determine the accuracy of each? Which do you trust more? Why? After your analysis and comparison, would you want to rephrase your prompt to the GenAI to direct it to a different output? How would you change your prompt and why?

For Discussion

1. With the general overview of AI's evolution provided in this chapter, discuss the ways in which that history does or does not affect your understanding of what AI and GenAI are and what they do.

2. AI and GenAI are applied in a wide range of places. In fact, it's almost impossible to avoid some interactions with AI. Discuss the ways in which you encounter AI most regularly.

03

INTEGRITY

LEARNING OBJECTIVES

▷ Recognize the tenets of "academic integrity."
▷ Understand the meanings of plagiarism.
▷ Describe the ways in which GenAI and plagiarism are connected.
▷ Employ citation styles for GenAI content.

BEFORE YOU READ THIS CHAPTER

There has been a lot of conversation about how GenAI might be used as a "cheater's tool" for completing writing assignments. From your experience in reading about, talking about, or hearing about GenAI platforms like ChatGPT, what do you think the role of GenAI will be in your own education, especially in writing?

INTRODUCTION

On May 12, 2023, *The Chronicle of Higher Education*—widely considered the primary news source for US higher education—published an essay in its "The Review/Opinion" section titled "I'm a Student. You Have No Idea How Much We're Using ChatGPT." Written by Columbia University undergraduate student Owen Kichizo Terry, the essay begins by saying, "Look at any high school or college academic integrity policy, and you'll find the same message: submit work that reflects your own thinking or face discipline. A year ago, this was just about the most common-sense rule on Earth. Today, it's laughably naive." He goes on to say, "In reality, it's very easy to use AI to do the lion's share of the thinking while still submitting work that looks like your own. Once this becomes clear, it follows that massive structural change is needed if our colleges are going to keep training students to think critically."[12] Terry claims that students use ChatGPT in ways that are undetectable and that point to a disconnect between how students use GenAI and how educators perceive that use.

When ChatGPT launched, the public conversation was rampant with claims that ChatGPT would ruin education because the machines would do all of the work for students. Because much of the panic about ChatGPT emerged from educators, who had been caught off guard by the new generative technologies, much of the conversation turned to plagiarism and other aspects of "academic integrity."

This chapter takes up questions about academic integrity and GenAI both conceptually—why and when using GenAI might be considered a violation of academic integrity—and in application—how we might ethically use GenAI in our own work.

ACADEMIC INTEGRITY

Before taking up the relationship between GenAI and academic integrity, let's consider the idea of academic integrity. Basically, integrity is about being honest and adhering to one's moral principles. For students, academic integrity is violated through such actions as plagiarism, cheating, contract cheating, and other forms of dishonesty. Academic integrity for faculty and administrators is similar, but can also require honesty and rigor in research and publication, as well as good conduct when teaching and assessing students.

Every academic institution has academic integrity policies. Some are for students and some for faculty and administrators. Interestingly, most academic integrity policies in the US grew not from the idea that faculty and administrators need to monitor students for acts of academic dishonesty, but from students themselves wanting to be sure that their work and the work of their classmates upheld the integrity of their colleges and universities. In the eighteenth century, there were only nine colleges in the US, and all of them developed academic honor codes which were monitored by the students enrolled in those schools. If someone violated the code, they would face the repercussions established by that community, which in some instances included expulsion. Honor codes were based, in part, on the desire to uphold ethical behavior on the part of all individual students as representatives of the campus community. Student oversight of these codes promoted student empowerment within the institution.

As more and more colleges and universities opened across the US, the role of these institutions shifted from primarily that of teaching students to more heavily emphasizing the production of original research. In this process, honor codes evolved to become more encompassing and to address academic integrity more broadly. Oversight extended to students in some matters, to faculty governing boards in others, and even to broader supervisory boards. Because professors need to maintain their reputations as researchers, teachers, and writers, academic integrity policies grew to encompass their work as well as students'. Concerns over intellectual property rights also contributed to our understanding of academic integrity, as those rights evolved to ensure that researchers didn't assume credit for the work of others or use others' research without acknowledging its influence. The importance of academic integrity increased as competition among research faculty increased, particularly in terms of funding and prestige.

Colleges and universities often require that statements about academic integrity appear on course syllabi, and at some institutions students are required to sign documents stating their compliance with honor codes.

PLAGIARISM

Academic integrity policies often specify exactly what a college or university means by plagiarism. Most often, we understand plagiarism to involve representing someone else's work or ideas as your own. Often this definition is expanded to identify different types of plagiarism, and some institutions identify as many as a dozen forms of plagiarism, among them

 ▷ **Direct plagiarism:** the word-for-word use of someone else's words or ideas without attribution of that work to the original writer/speaker/ thinker.

 ▷ **Duplicate plagiarism** (sometimes called self-plagiarism): the reuse of work you submitted for evaluation in another class without direct permission from the instructor to do so. This can include resubmitting entire assignments or parts of previous assignments.

 ▷ **Patchwork plagiarism** (sometimes called mosaic plagiarism): the rewording of someone else's words or ideas and combining them with someone else's words, creating a mosaic or quilt of ideas from others in order to create the appearance of original thought or writing.

 ▷ **Paraphrasing plagiarism:** using someone else's words or ideas but changing a few words, often replacing words with synonyms, in an attempt to make the material not appear like the original. This is a very common form of plagiarism.

 ▷ **Accidental plagiarism:** the inadvertent act of plagiarism due to a lack of awareness of how to cite sources or a lack of awareness that the information or language used in an assignment response was initially produced by another.

Many colleges and universities include in their academic integrity policies statements about the reasons students may cheat or plagiarize. Most commonly, those reasons include the hope to improve a grade, a fear of failing, or poor time management.

However, there are two other reasons why students may plagiarize that are quite telling. First, many students cheat or plagiarize because of lack of investment in the assignment. This occurs most often in required classes in which students have little interest. It can also occur when a particular assignment is uninteresting or unmotivating, even if the student is invested in the subject area. While the blame for plagiarism cannot and should not be redirected to the instructor or the assignment—it's always the student's choice to plagiarize—this is one reason for teachers to develop dynamic, engaging assignments.

Provocation

Chapter 2 provides an abbreviated explanation as to how GenAI technologies work. It describes the process by which a GenAI is given a prompt, scrubs through the information in the LLMs it has access to, and then reorganizes that information into what it predicts to be the anticipated response. One might argue that this process is also how humans do things. For example, if we are given a writing assignment in a class, we scrub through everything we already know about the subject: all of our experiences, our stored thoughts, our memories, and everything else in our personal databases. Some of this we do intentionally and consciously; some of it we do tacitly. We then reorganize that information into an output that we predict is what the instructor wants as an output.

Some claim that every GenAI output is inherently plagiarism, on grounds that everything the GenAI creates was originally someone else's words or thoughts. Yet, similarly, most of what we say, write, and think could be argued to be plagiarism, because we so often cull it, reorder it, and re-present it from other peoples' ideas and expressions. Each sentence, each word, and each claim I make in this book is arguably a reorganization of what I've learned from others.

First, consider the ramifications of this on how we think about things like individuality, sense of self, expression, creativity, and even intelligence. Second, consider how such an acknowledgement of the similarities between GenAI and human thinking might affect what we understand about plagiarism and academic integrity.

Second, many students plagiarize inadvertently because they don't understand what plagiarism is or what the policies of their institutions are. Many international students are identified as plagiarizing simply because they are unfamiliar with North American plagiarism policies and citation practices. Others, both international and domestic, receive inadequate instruction as to when and how citation must be included.

The seemingly sudden appearance of accessible GenAI technologies compels higher education to rethink many of its fundamental assumptions and beliefs, including what we mean by plagiarism. Traditionally, we understood plagiarism to mean using the words or ideas of another person without crediting that work to its author. This understanding of plagiarism has been so central to the core values of higher education that it spawned detailed methods and expectations for research and source citation. There would be no need for APA, MLA, Chicago, Turabian, IEEE, and other citation styles were it not for this classic understanding of plagiarism and academic integrity. However, the emergence of GenAI calls into question this understanding in three critical ways:

1. The customary understanding holds that plagiarism occurs only when a person "steals" ideas or words from another person. However, with GenAI, the output cannot be attributed to anyone other than the AI. We may need to rethink plagiarism in terms of *artifact*—the thing from which information can be plagiarized—instead of *author*. This also raises questions about intellectual property ownership, which get bound up in ideologies of capital and property.

2. The quandaries surrounding plagiarism and GenAI technologies also call into question our longstanding belief that humans are the only entities that can operate as authors. Now that GenAI technologies can "write" independently, are we willing to grant them authorial agency (and even copyright ownership) over the texts they produce? If a GenAI is prompted to write a short story, is the GenAI the "author" of that story in the same way as a person would be? What about a painting, or a photograph?

3. Because GenAI provides output based upon its LLM—which comprises data that humans and machines have written—we must ask: do GenAI platforms themselves commit plagiarism, regardless of how their output is used? Can non-humans commit plagiarism?

How do we understand and learn to use GenAI given of our current definitions of plagiarism, and how should we adjust our understanding of plagiarism in the shadow of GenAI?

For now, teachers and administrators—and most students surveyed—identify copying text from a GenAI's output as equivalent to copying from another student. Longer term, however, instructors, researchers, administrators, and students may need to reassess and redefine plagiarism and academic honesty, especially if GenAI technologies become more integrated into many people's writing processes (both students and professionals).

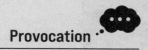

Provocation

Just as educational institutions will need to rethink plagiarism and academic integrity in the shadow of GenAI, industry will need to address similar concerns. Consider, for example, a magazine or blog in the recreational industry that uses a GenAI platform to write an article about advances in the thermoplastic elastomers used to make hiking shoes. Assume that the topic of the article is timely and important to the industry, and that competing publications have also generated similar articles using the same GenAI application. Since the GenAI has scrubbed its data from an LLM, the articles in each publication will inevitably be similar in the content they convey and perhaps even in their writing style. How will industry develop its policies of professional integrity in light of this possibility? And how will the "writers" who use GenAI to produce such content be trained in doing so?

SHOW YOUR WORK

Many people have referred to the "scrub" segment of the GenAI process as a "black box," a system in which we can see what the inputs are and what the outcomes are, but cannot see what happens in the process leading from input to output.

In many academic disciplines, students are asked to show their work, demonstrating that they understand the processes for getting from point A to point B. For example, a math teacher might assign students ten equations or proofs to solve, but if the students just submit the answers to each, whether they are correct or not, the teacher may not accept the responses because the expectation is for students to show their work, to demonstrate that they understand *how* to solve the problem. In many science classes,

"I THINK YOU SHOULD BE MORE EXPLICIT HERE IN STEP TWO."

students are asked to show their work so as to indicate their mastery of the process of actually conducting scientific experiments.

In the 1970s, composition scholars began to study the processes by which writers produce writing, and they developed the idea of the writing process—commonly identified as prewriting, researching, drafting, revising content, revising organization, editing, proofreading, and lastly publishing or submission. The idea was that if instructors could teach students a reliable process, then the students could use that process in any situation where they had to write: their classes, their jobs, their civic lives, and their personal lives. Focusing on the writing process shifted attention from the written product to the processes by which the product is created.

"Show your work" has been a mantra in education for a long time, but as of now, GenAI cannot show its work. A GenAI cannot perform the act of drafting and revising or returning multiple drafts of, say, an essay that improves from early drafts to later drafts. Nor can it explain how it wrote what it wrote. Thus, simply giving a GenAI a prompt or assignment to complete and asking it to solve the problem or write the essay is not likely to fulfill the intention of the assignment. Likewise, doing so ignores the purpose of the assignment and the learning experience the assignment is designed to provide. Other more collaborative approaches to using GenAI in writing may be less problematic in this respect (see Chapter 4).

CITATION

The fundamental, baseline principles for academic integrity and the use of GenAI must always be **transparency** and **documentation.**

Citation is designed to allow a reader to locate the source that an author uses, both to double-check the accuracy of the author's use and to conduct further research. However, GenAI-produced content is non-recoverable. If you ask a GenAI platform to write a document for you, that document is not normally stored in any publicly accessible format. As a result, a reader can't examine the source of a cited GenAI output as they could with a cited journal article, book, or web page.

That said, it's still important to account for the use of GenAI-generated content as a matter of integrity and transparency. Most of the standard citation manuals and style guides have developed citation approaches for GenAI content. Here are the recommendations of a few leading style guides.

MLA

The Modern Language Association states that writers should

▷ cite a generative AI tool whenever you paraphrase, quote, or incorporate into your own work any content (whether text, image, data, or other) that was created by it

▷ acknowledge all functional uses of the tool (like editing your prose or translating words) in a note, your text, or another suitable location

▷ take care to vet the secondary sources it cites [13]

The MLA then provides this approach to an MLA template for citing GenAI content:

Author
We do not recommend treating the AI tool as an author. This recommendation follows the policies developed by various publishers, including the MLA's journal *PMLA.*

Title of Source
Describe what was generated by the AI tool. This may involve

including information about the prompt in the Title of Source element if you have not done so in the text.

Title of Container
Use the Title of Container element to name the AI tool (e.g., *ChatGPT*).

Version
Name the version of the AI tool as specifically as possible. For example, the examples in this post were developed using *ChatGPT* 3.5, which assigns a specific date to the version, so the Version element shows this version date.

Publisher
Name the company that made the tool.

Date
Give the date the content was generated.

Location
Give the general URL for the tool.[14]

The MLA gives the following example of how to cite a GenAI source in a Works Cited list:

"Describe the symbolism of the green light in the book *The Great Gatsby* by F. Scott Fitzgerald" prompt. *ChatGPT*, 13 Feb. version, OpenAI, 8 Mar. 2023, chat.openai.com/chat.[15]

APA

The Publication Manual of the American Psychological Association notes that GenAI chat sessions and outputs

are not retrievable by other readers, and although nonretrievable data or quotations in APA Style papers are usually cited as personal communications, with ChatGPT-generated text there is no person communicating. Quoting ChatGPT's text from a chat session is therefore more like sharing an algorithm's output;

thus, credit the author of the algorithm with a reference list entry and the corresponding in-text citation.[16]

The APA offers this example:

> When prompted with "Is the left brain right brain divide real or a metaphor?" the ChatGPT-generated text indicated that although the two brain hemispheres are somewhat specialized, "the notation that people can be characterized as 'left-brained' or 'right-brained' is considered to be an oversimplification and a popular myth" (OpenAI, 2023).
>
> **Reference**
> OpenAI. (2023). *ChatGPT* (Mar 14 version) [Large language model]. https://chat.openai.com/chat[17]

The APA notes that you may wish to include the complete text of any long GenAI output as an appendix.

IEEE

The Institute of Electrical and Electronics Engineers style guide does not provide guidelines for nonrecoverable materials such as GenAI. However, they do provide guidelines for citing private communications, and many institutions recommend this approach for citing GenAI in IEEE-formatted documents.

> [#] Reference number (matching the in-text citation number)
> Author(s) name
> private communication
> Abbreviated month and year or correspondence
> [1] H. Shi, private communication, Apr. 2022.[18]

Thus, a GenAI output would be cited this way:

> ChatGPT, chat output, Apr. 2022.

Note that IEEE, unlike MLA, does identify the GenAI as one would an author.

END OF CHAPTER MATERIALS

So What?

1. So what if you plagiarize? So what if you use GenAI without citation? What would be the likely outcome—in terms of academic and social integrity and student learning—if we had no restrictions on these practices?

2. As noted earlier, there is a historical distinction between academic honor codes (enforced by students themselves) and institutionally imposed policies (enforced by faculty and administrators). So what? Do such distinctions in origins and administration matter?

Conceptual AI

1. The idea that ChatGPT and other GenAI platforms are "cheaters' tools" is prevalent in popular conversations about GenAI. However, every technology has the potential to be used in nefarious ways, no matter the intent of its design and its anticipated use. There are countless examples of technologies that were designed to have positive impacts but which, intentionally or unintentionally, have been used for corrupt or destructive purposes. Given this, and given the worry over how students will use GenAI to cheat, how might we come to terms with GenAI as a technology with the potential for positive or negative effects?

2. It *is* stated in this chapter that students have a tendency to "cheat" on assignments when they have little interest or investment. Do you believe this is true? In what ways might GenAI exacerbate student cheating in such contexts? Are there any ways in which it might actually discourage cheating?

3. Is it plagiarism to include written output from a GenAI platform in an assignment without citation? Is it plagiarism to use a GenAI-produced image without identifying it as such? Is there a relevant moral difference between textual and visual use? If so, what is it?

4. Recall the opinion essay by Columbia University undergraduate student Owen Kichizo Terry at the start of this chapter. In that same essay, Terry goes on to write:

The common fear among teachers is that AI is actually writing our essays for us, but that isn't what happens. You can hand ChatGPT a prompt and ask it for a finished product, but you'll probably get an essay with a very general claim, middle-school-level sentence structure, and half as many words as you wanted. The more effective, and increasingly popular, strategy is to have the AI walk you through the writing process step by step. You tell the algorithm what your topic is and ask for a central claim, then have it give you an outline to argue this claim. Depending on the topic, you might even be able to have it write each paragraph the outline calls for, one by one, then rewrite them yourself to make them flow better.

Is the process Terry describes plagiarism? Is it a violation of academic integrity?

5. When you write, it's likely that you already use some AI tools such as spell checkers and grammar checkers. These tools have altered our learning in many ways. You no longer need to know how to spell every word correctly. You no longer *need* to know all of the rules of grammar. Is using these kinds of tools a violation of academic integrity? Write a short essay comparing the accepted use of AI tools such as spelling and grammar checkers with the often-prohibited use of GenAI.

Applied AI

1. Ask a GenAI program to define plagiarism. How does it respond to prompts asking if GenAI use is a violation of academic integrity?

2. How might you use GenAI without violating your institution's academic integrity policies? Using ChatGPT or any other text-generating GenAI that you have access to, develop an ethical approach to using GenAI that is compatible with your institution's academic integrity policies.

3. Locate your institution's academic integrity policies. Then, using ChatGPT or any other text-generating GenAI, write a prompt to produce a comprehensive policy for academic integrity and GenAI use for a college or university. How does the GenAI response compare with your institution's policies?

4. Several media sites have published guides on how to use GenAI to cheat without getting caught. Prompt ChatGPT (or any other text-producing GenAI platform) to provide detailed instructions about how to use the platform for academic assignments without detection. Are the instructions compatible with your institution's academic integrity policies? Could the instructions be modified so as to be made compatible (for example, by requiring citations of all GenAI content)?

For Discussion

1. For many years, teachers have been using detection programs like TurnItIn to identify whether a student has submitted plagiarized work. Such detection programs rely on non-generative AI, and each time a student's paper is submitted, it is added to the AI's LLM. Is there any inconsistency in allowing AI for this purpose but prohibiting students from using it to complete assignments?

2. Imagine a student who is enrolled in a writing-intensive class but for whom English is a second language. When given a writing prompt as an essay assignment, the student thinks through the prompt in their native language, takes notes in their native language, and then drafts and revises the essay in their native language. The student then uses a translation tool such as Google Translate—a form of Natural Language Processing AI—to convert the essay into English. The student then edits and proofreads the essay in its English form and submits it. Is this student's use of technology a violation of academic integrity?

   Next, consider a native English-speaking student in the same class, who has been given the same assignment but is unable to think of a good idea for an essay. They use GenAI to generate ideas and create an outline, and then use this as a starting point to write their essay. Is this a violation of academic integrity?

   Lastly, consider another student in the same class, who similarly has difficulty coming up with an idea. They use a search engine to learn more about the subject and to see what others have written about it. The student uses this information to help choose a topic, and then they write their essay. Is this a violation of academic integrity?

   What are the relevant differences and similarities among these situations?

3. Is monitoring for plagiarism an act of policing or an act of education?

PART II

Opportunities and Applications

04

WRITING WITH GenAI

LEARNING OBJECTIVES

▷ Use GenAI in prewriting.
▷ Use GenAI in conducting research and in citation.
▷ Compose drafts using GenAI.
▷ Use GenAI as a revision tool.
▷ Use GenAI as an editing/proofreading tool.
▷ Evaluate the benefits and drawbacks of using GenAI when writing.

BEFORE YOU READ THIS CHAPTER

Before reading more about how to use GenAI in your writing, think about the ways in which you already rely on AI and GenAI to complete your academic writing assignments and the writing you produce in other contexts.

INTRODUCTION

This chapter examines *practical* approaches for writing with GenAI. It examines when and how to integrate GenAI into your own writing processes, or how to write *with* AI. There are many potential benefits to writing with GenAI; efficiency and timesaving are two of the most often cited. Remember, as discussed in Chapter 3, that one of the common reasons students cheat on assignments is poor time management. GenAI can reduce the amount of time required to complete a writing assignment.

While ChatGPT is what brought GenAI as a writing tool to the attention of the public, other free and subscription-based writing-focused GenAI platforms are also available. Notably, Grammarly boasts that it can provide AI assistance with grammar, spelling, style, and tone. The subscription platform Wordtune offers similar resources but also includes AI assistance with invention and arrangement.

Keep in mind that, as we saw in Chapters 2 and 3, there are multiple reasons—integrity and hallucinations key among them—why using GenAI can be risky. Instead of advocating wholesale use of GenAI as a replacement for human authorship, this chapter encourages human–machine collaborations. It also emphasizes the need for a human author to confirm the accuracy and relevance of all GenAI-produced content and the importance of ethical considerations at all stages of the writing process. The human author must be the primary author. Remember that the word 'author' is derived from the same root as 'authority,' and to claim to be a document's author implies that you maintain authority over that document.

INVENTION AND PREWRITING

The writing process begins with "prewriting," a name for all of the activities one undertakes before the actual writing. Prewriting is a critical part of the process, yet for many people it's the most difficult one simply because it's so often hard to get started on any writing task.

Long before writing instructors began formally teaching "the writing process," classical rhetoricians identified the five canons of rhetoric—a means of categorizing the steps a speaker or writer needs to take in order to produce oration or writing. These canons are invention, arrangement, style, memory, and delivery. In about 50 BCE, the Roman orator and lawyer Cicero organized the five canons of rhetoric into a usable, teachable system in his book *De Inventione*, and then, about 150 years later, the Roman rhetorician Quintillian expanded our understanding of the five canons in his massive twelve-volume book *Institutio Oratoria* (which is a lot like a contemporary textbook). The five canons of rhetoric became so influential in how we think about and teach writing that they are now cornerstones of our contemporary understanding of the writing process.

The five canons begin with *Inventio* (invention), which we understand as the part of writing when we "invent" the ideas and arguments we will use. Much of invention begins through thinking. We think about what our writing task is; we think about what the writing assignment means; and we think about what we think the teacher who assigned it wants us to do. We also think about our own motivations for responding to the assignment: what interests us about the assignment? What confuses us? What do we know about the assignment and what don't we know? We also think about the audience we will write for and how that affects what and how we will write. Often, a significant part of prewriting involves reading what others have said or written about the subject in order to trigger our own thoughts and to familiarize ourselves with the main ideas and conversations surrounding a subject.

Prewriting is also the phase of the writing process in which you begin to hone your thinking about a subject into a specific thesis that can be addressed thoroughly but not uncontrollably. Prewriting helps you focus your ideas into something manageable. There are many methods for prewriting: reading, discussing, listing, note-taking, brainstorming, outlining, journaling, mind-mapping, and freewriting, for example. More recently, web searches and resources such as Wikipedia have become popular approaches to prewriting.

GenAI is another powerful tool that can assist with prewriting. It would be foolish to abandon the tried-and-true prewriting strategies you already employ, but consider how GenAI can enhance those strategies.

Depending on your instructor's and institution's policies, consider using GenAI in these ways when prewriting:

▷ **Generate ideas:** You can prompt GenAI to provide multiple perspectives on a given subject; it can provide alternate viewpoints you may have overlooked as you think through an assignment.

▷ **Inspiration:** Just getting started can be the hardest part of responding to a writing assignment. Writer's block, lack of interest, or even just a lack of understanding can leave writers unable to begin. Ask a GenAI to provide an opening sentence for your assignment and then try writing the next sentence yourself.

▷ **Discussion:** Talking through an assignment can be helpful, but sometimes finding the right person to talk to is difficult. Your roommates, family members, and friends might not be in the same course, and might not have any interest in your subject. GenAI—specifically chatbots such as ChatGPT—can engage with you in conversations so as to help you work through your ideas on the subject.

▷ **Direction:** GenAI can help you locate key writers and positions on the subject you wish to write about. It can direct you to texts already written about the subject. It can identify the primary players in conversations about the subject. Ask a GenAI to identify the most important articles written about your subject, and then read those articles.

RESEARCH

Most academic writing requires some degree of research. Academic disciplines generally understand **research** to mean systematic examinations and studies of available information. While that broad understanding might be applicable across disciplines, every discipline has its own approach to research. Understanding and employing research methodologies within specific disciplinary contexts is critical. Research in the humanities is different from research in the social sciences, which is different from research in natural sciences, computer sciences, the arts, and so on. In the humanities, for example, research might involve reading critiques of Herman Melville's *Moby-Dick*. Research in pharmaceuticals might involve administering a new drug and monitoring the physiological effects it has on a group of test subjects. In most writing-intensive courses—the kinds of courses for which this book is primarily designed—research involves engaging previously published texts and using information in those texts to support your own ideas.

GenAI can be a useful research assistant, but recognize that research assistants don't make the decisions about what research to use or the value of that research. So, if you use GenAI to assist you, remember that you still need to do the work of confirming the accuracy and value of the research the GenAI returns.

GenAI can direct you to relevant information, identify important sources for further reading, and direct you to pertinent conversations about a given topic. It can also summarize key points of research. Such summaries can be useful in synthesizing large bodies of information or gaining a better understanding of a subject or text. However, as noted above, GenAI is susceptible to hallucinations; so you will always want to confirm the validity of such summaries.

There is discussion now about how GenAI might overtake or synthesize with traditional web searches as the primary method for identifying resources about a given subject. A standard search engine will only return a list of items that match the given search terms, whereas a GenAI will also summarize and synthesize that information.

You must be cautious about a few things when using GenAI to assist with research:

▷ Any given GenAI platform can only provide research information from data to which it has access within its Large Language Model, and all LLMs have various limitations (see Chapter 2). Therefore, any given GenAI is inherently limited. You should not assume that GenAI output in response to a research question is comprehensive.

▷ The LLMs of many GenAI platforms take time to update and may include only dated information on a given topic. Using outdated information may reduce the relevance and accuracy of your work.

▷ GenAI research can be limited by the biases built into its system (see Chapter 9).

▷ GenAI is notorious for returning hallucinations, particularly in written responses (see Chapter 2). While this is currently a serious problem, it's also one of the areas in which GenAI is rapidly improving. Anticipate that GenAI hallucinations will appear less often as time goes by, but be aware that you should confirm every piece of information GenAI returns to you.

▷ GenAI does not understand context, so it may return information that is relevant in other contexts but not relevant to your subject.

Citation

The reason for citation is to allow a reader to trace information back to its original source. Citation is crucial to academic integrity in writing because it

- ▷ provides a guide to how you contextualize your arguments and information

- ▷ shows that you understand how not to plagiarize

- ▷ acknowledges credit and shows that you understand from where you draw your ideas

- ▷ adds credibility to your work by situating it among the peer-reviewed work that came before

GenAI can help us to automate the processes for gathering and cataloging citation information about other sources used in our research. Early iterations of GenAI didn't readily provide source data on the information used to generate an output. However, newer versions of ChatGPT and other writing GenAI platforms such as Wordtune are becoming more adept at providing citations. Continued use of GenAI in academic settings—both classroom and faculty research—will likely lead to further improvement in this arena.

DRAFTING

Remember that GenAI does not provide multiple drafts; it cannot describe how it got from A (the prompt you provide) to B (the output it returns in response to the prompt). *Its* writing process is not *your* writing process.

A student might prompt a GenAI to "write a 1,000-word essay about *Moby-Dick*." Such a prompt is generic and will return a broad and bland response from GenAI that will fail to say anything interesting. When an instructor provides a writing assignment, they normally expect students to return a piece of writing that is more expansive and specific than the assignment itself. Attempting to use GenAI by simply plugging in an assignment instruction as a prompt doesn't typically produce viable work, because the output fails to meet the expectations of the instructor.

There are three important points to consider:

1. Don't use GenAI to draft an entire written response. Instead, use GenAI to provide ideas for limited parts of your draft that you can then incorporate into a larger whole. For example, if you've been assigned to write an essay about *Moby-Dick,* and you've decided that the first part of the essay will provide biographical information about Herman Melville, begin by asking GenAI to provide specific facts about Melville: date of birth, home, education, career, etc. (be sure to confirm all information for accuracy). GenAI can be more useful and more detailed when your prompts ask for *details* rather than complete texts.

2. Revise your prompts. GenAI works best when you engage with it over multiple prompts, teaching it to give you the outputs you are actually looking for. If the GenAI provides biographical information on Melville that focuses primarily on his personal life, and your intention is to write exclusively about his literary career, tell this to the GenAI. Continue to refine your prompts until the output is useful for your purposes.

3. Outputs should *inform* your drafting; they should not themselves be your drafts. Remember that GenAI does not "draft" per se. It provides a response to a prompt—a product, not a process.

Even if the draft is informed by GenAI output, it should reflect your thoughts, your writing style, and your objectives in responding to the assignment. Rather than starting with a GenAI output and supplementing it with your own ideas, begin by drafting your ideas and then use GenAI to help flesh out your writing.

Arrangement is another of the five canons of rhetoric. It refers to how you organize the information in a document. How you arrange the content of your writing depends on your objectives as well as the kind of document you're writing. For example, when writing a traditional academic essay, you might begin with an introduction, and follow that with paragraphs delivering information on specific examples, organized from most important to least important. In writing the script for a podcast, on the other hand, you might arrange information in such a way that the most important detail isn't revealed until the end. Prompting a GenAI platform to check the organization of your writing and suggest alternative arrangements can be exceptionally helpful. GenAI can also be useful in synthesizing and organizing large pieces of writing into a single, fluid document. GenAI can take the various parts of a draft and help you combine and organize them into a cohesive document.

Predictive Text

GenAI can also be a powerful tool for drafting individual sentences and selecting words in your writing. Predictive text is a feature of word processors such as Microsoft Word, as well as text messaging systems and some social media platforms. Predictive text is a type of GenAI that anticipates the most likely letter or word to follow the letter or word you are typing by identifying patterns within its LLM and suggesting what you're likely to type next based on those repeated patterns in other writing. Predictive text can speed up typing by reducing the number of keystrokes you have to make. It can also be valuable in suggesting language that resonates with readers.

The same functions that drive predictive text also work with spell checkers and grammar checkers, which can offer corrections and suggestions. Given the emphasis on grammatical correctness in academic writing, these kinds of predictive GenAI features can help better align your writing with academic (as well as professional and civic) expectations.

Provocation

In what ways have spell checkers and grammar checkers changed how students write? If you were asked to produce a document but weren't permitted to use a grammar checker, how would your writing differ from the writing you produce in Microsoft Word or through applications such as Grammarly? Has an instructor ever told you that you can't use spell checkers or grammar checkers? Do students need to know grammatical rules at all? Why or why not? In what ways have these tools changed what we need to know about writing?

REVISING

Revision can be thought of as the process of making big changes to a document. The smaller stuff—such as fixing grammar mistakes—can be addressed later, in editing (see the next section). Revision is the part of the writing process to which writers should be most attentive. It should usually take more time than any other part of the process. Revising is an activity that could often go on endlessly. But in order to actually complete writing tasks, writers need to exercise discipline so as to stop when a piece of writing has met its objectives.

GenAI can provide useful insights into how you might revise a document. However, to do so effectively, you'll need to provide multiple prompts to guide the GenAI toward the outcomes you wish to achieve. Simply telling a GenAI to "revise this essay" won't provide the bot with enough information on what sorts of revisions you wish it to make.

Style is another of the five canons of rhetoric. Style can be thought of as the choices you make that help connect your writing to your reader. These include choices about wording, sentence structure, and tone that influence how readers "hear" your writing.

GenAI tools can help writers adjust their style in several ways. Most commonly, they can

▷ ensure that the style is consistent throughout a piece of writing
▷ change text from one style to another
▷ suggest ways to improve the style of a document

Consider the following example of a paragraph written for an academic assignment about the importance of digital literacy. The paragraph is human-written in a formal, academic style:

Digital literacy is a crucial skill set in today's rapidly advancing technological landscape. It encompasses the ability to effectively navigate, evaluate, and utilize digital tools and resources for various purposes. Digital literacy is not merely limited to technical proficiency; it encompasses critical thinking, information literacy, and ethical considerations. To be digitally literate means to possess the knowledge and skills necessary to responsibly engage with digital media and technology. It empowers individuals to critically assess the credibility of online information, discern between reliable and misleading sources, and protect their privacy and security in the digital realm. Furthermore, digital literacy equips individuals with the capacity to create, collaborate, and communicate in a digital environment, fostering innovation and productivity. In an increasingly interconnected world, digital literacy serves as a gateway to opportunity, enabling individuals to actively participate in the digital age and make informed decisions.

Prompted to "revise this paragraph into an informal style," one GenAI returned this revision:

Hey, being good with tech is super important these days, what with everything moving so fast. It's all about knowing your way around digital stuff, figuring out what's good and what's not, and using it all for whatever you need. But it's not just about being a tech whiz. You've gotta think critically, know how to find and use info, and be aware of the ethics involved. Being digitally savvy means you've got the know-how to use digital media and tech in a responsible way. It helps you figure out what's legit online, spot the fakes, and keep your personal stuff safe. Plus, it gives you the skills to make, share, and chat in the digital world, which can really boost your creativity and productivity. In a world where everything's connected, being digitally savvy opens doors. It lets you get involved in the digital age and make smart choices.[19]

While this revision for style might seem a bit over-the-top, it's indicative of the kinds of stylistic revisions GenAI can provide. Honing the prompt and providing multiple prompts may lead to a more desirable result. Here's a further revision, with the GenAI prompted to "revise the paragraph again, making it less wordy and more professional yet still informal."

Being tech-savvy is key in our fast-paced digital world. It's more than just knowing your way around gadgets; it's about critical thinking, finding reliable info, and understanding digital ethics. If you're digitally literate, you can responsibly use tech, spot fake news, and protect your online privacy. Plus, it gives you the tools to create, collaborate, and communicate digitally. In our interconnected world, digital literacy isn't just a nice-to-have, it's a must-have. It's your ticket to actively participate in the digital age and make smart decisions.[20]

Perhaps one of the most beneficial ways GenAI can assist in revision is by providing feedback. However, simply asking GenAI to provide feedback on a piece of writing without specific instructions can be fruitless. Think about all of those times you asked a friend, classmate, roommate, or family member to read something you wrote for a school assignment, hoping they'd help you revise it, where they simply responded with "It's good." Without prompts, other people aren't likely to know what to look for. The same is true for GenAI.

There are many specific elements of writing you can prompt GenAI to examine. Consider the following prompts:

▷ Does the writing meet the goal of the assignment?
▷ If the desired audience is [define the audience, i.e., college students or marketing managers, etc.], is the tone, content, format, and organization appropriate for that audience?
▷ Is the content focused?
▷ Is the argument well-reasoned?
▷ Does the evidence support the thesis?
▷ Is the information well-developed and thorough?
▷ Is any critical information missing?
▷ Are the sources cited correctly in [provide style guide—MLA, APA]?
▷ Is the included information synthesized within the context of the thesis?
▷ Is the information presented logically?
▷ Is the information presented clearly?
▷ Does the introduction clearly introduce the content of the thesis?
▷ Is the introduction engaging?
▷ Is the thesis statement clear and evident?
▷ Does the writing convey its purpose clearly?
▷ Are the paragraphs organized logically?
▷ Is each paragraph cohesive?
▷ Is the purpose of each paragraph clear?
▷ Do the headings match the content of each section?
▷ Are the topic sentences clear?

▷ Do the transitions between paragraphs make clear the connections between the paragraphs?
▷ Does the conclusion end the document clearly?

EDITING AND PROOFREADING

Whereas revision focuses on large elements such as content and organization, editing and proofreading focus on details such as sentence-level structure, grammar, punctuation, and spelling. Editing and proofreading are usually the last part of the process, though most writers incorporate editing throughout their writing work. It's easy to correct the spelling of a word as soon as the spell checker identifies an error, and trying intentionally to ignore the checker's flags is silly. So, though formally understood as the final stage of the writing process, editing and proofreading are often synthesized throughout.

Technically, editing and proofreading are not the same thing, though writers—especially writers who are operating under deadlines—often conflate the two. Editing involves making your writing more readable. This can include improving clarity and concision, and correcting wordiness. Proofreading involves correcting your writing in terms of formal rules, such as those of verb construction, punctuation, grammar, and spelling.

Proofreading issues can be addressed using the GenAI tools built into word processors such as Microsoft Word. However, using another GenAI platform—like ChatGPT, Wordtune, or Grammarly—to proofread and edit drafts can help you further hone the correctness and readability of a document.

For example, GenAI tools can provide suggestions for refining word choice. Student writers frequently repeat words or use the same verbs too frequently. Repetition of a word in a written document can start to weigh on how a reader "hears" the voice of the document. One way to check for word repetition is to use a word processor's search function. Consider this paragraph:

Digital writing is a dynamic and ever-evolving medium that is revolutionizing the way we communicate. It is a vast landscape where words come alive in the digital realm. The essence of digital writing is captured in its interactivity, where readers can engage, comment, and share their thoughts in real-time. It is a medium that is accessible and inclusive, reaching audiences across the globe with a click of a button. Digital writing is a powerful tool for collaboration, where multiple voices can merge seamlessly in a virtual space. It is a platform that is constantly evolving, adapting to new technologies and trends, pushing the boundaries of creativity and expression.

Repeating the verb "is" nine times in six sentences may be grammatically correct, but it can make reading the text cumbersome. A GenAI can help identify repetition if prompted to do so. GenAI platforms can also make suggestions as to more dynamic verbs. But be careful, as this can lead to some pretty odd suggestions:

> Digital writing thrives as a dynamic and perpetually morphing medium, overhauling the way we communicate. It unfolds as a vast landscape where words ignite in the digital realm. The essence of digital writing gets seized in its interactivity, where readers can dive in, annotate, and broadcast their thoughts in real-time. It stands as a medium that's open and inclusive, touching audiences across the globe with a tap of a button. Digital writing serves as a potent instrument for collaboration, where multiple voices can fuse flawlessly in a virtual space. It persists as a platform that's ceaselessly metamorphosing, conforming to new technologies and trends, shattering the boundaries of creativity and expression.[21]

So consider, alternatively, using the word suggestions offered by a thesaurus (there's one built into Microsoft Word). Remember, too, that you should understand the nuances of a word's meaning before simply adding it to your writing.

There are many ways to prompt a GenAI to edit and proofread. Consider these prompts:

▷ Check for grammar
▷ Check for spelling
▷ Suggest better wording and sentence structure
▷ Check for tone—formal, informal, etc.

▷   Check for consistency in style
▷   Check for over-used words
▷   Check for passive sentence construction

CLIMBING MOUNT EVEREST

In college, instructors ask students to write to demonstrate what they've learned (the content of the writing) and to show that they know how to communicate what they've learned (the form of the writing). Extensive use of GenAI may circumvent some of the intended outcomes, such as learning how to perform each part of the writing process. However, in some contexts—especially professional ones—learning isn't an intended outcome of writing, and completion of the task is what matters most.

GenAI expert Cath Ellis argued in a recent webinar that the difference between using GenAI and not using GenAI can be thought of as the difference between climbing Mount Everest and taking a helicopter to the top.[22] Certainly, you *could* take a helicopter to the top of the mountain successfully and could then truthfully say that you've been to the top of Everest. But there's difference in the experience of taking the helicopter versus climbing to the top.

The helicopter passenger won't have as intimate a knowledge of the mountain as the climber, but they will have completed the task in a fraction of the time. The climber will leave the mountain with an expansive skill set for climbing, and with each subsequent climb will become even more adept. But the labor to develop that skill set is the result of a desire to learn that skill set. The helicopter passenger likely started with a vastly different objective—perhaps they only wished to see the view from the summit as quickly as possible, or perhaps they were conducting a scientific experiment at the summit and had no particular interest in the experience or process of climbing. Keep in mind, too, that the helicopter passenger doesn't get to the top of Everest independently. They require great resources, including access to the helicopter and to someone whose own skill set involves flying a helicopter in dangerous conditions.

The helicopter path to the top of Everest might be a useful metaphor for using GenAI to write. Whichever path you take, the task can be completed; but what you gain from each is fundamentally different. Depending on your purpose, either can be preferable. While the climber may consider the passenger to have cheated their way up, the passenger may consider the climber to be inefficient in reaching the top. There are some contexts where learning the skills to climb Everest is most valuable and there are others where reaching the top most efficiently (and learning the skills required to commission a helicopter) is more important. When considering the use of GenAI in your own writing, you'll need to consider the context of the task, as well as the ethical and policy considerations involved.

END OF CHAPTER MATERIALS

So What?

1. GenAI can be quite beneficial to the efficiency of one's writing, but it also comes with many drawbacks. So what? Do the benefits outweigh the drawbacks?

2. Many educators hold that a major benefit of writing assignments is that they can help students learn to solve difficult problems and better articulate their own ideas. Does the use of GenAI change that? So what does that matter?

Conceptual AI

1. Part of this chapter addresses the ways in which GenAI can be used to address stylistic and grammatical correctness through tools such as spell checkers, grammar checkers, and synonym providers. In the past, demonstrating correctness was an important part of showing proficiency in writing. But if correctness can—for the most part—be addressed through GenAI, does that affect the need for writers to learn rules of grammar and spelling?

2. We often think of written work as a reflection of the writer and their ability. Instructors use writing to judge how well a student knows a subject and how well they can articulate information on that subject. This is also why, when someone shares a piece of writing with some-one else, they often worry: "Are they going to think I'm stupid?" If you use GenAI to produce a piece of writing, how does this reflect on you as a writer? Does the use of GenAI change the relationship between the writer and their writing? If a writer you respect were to publicly

announce that they use GenAI, would this alter your perception of them?

3. Create a document describing the pros and cons of using GenAI in writing. Include a mix of text and visual material.

Applied AI

1. Examine a writing assignment you've received in the past. Use a search engine to identify several relevant sources that you would most likely use to complete the assignment. Then, using a GenAI platform, generate a list of relevant sources for the same assignment, including summaries of each source. How do the outputs of the search engine and the GenAI compare in terms of usefulness, accuracy, and timeliness? How can you revise each query to hone the responses to your specific needs?

2. Using the strategies described in this chapter, use a GenAI platform to revise a document you've already submitted as a school or work assignment. Do the GenAI's suggestions help, and if so, in what ways?

3. Using GenAI at all stages of the writing process—from invention to editing—write a traditional academic essay about how to use GenAI in college writing assignments.

For Discussion

1. While instructors often emphasize the writing process as a manageable way for students to approach writing assignments, most students—and most writers, in general—use hybrid and adjusted versions of "the writing process" when they actually write. In fact, it may be more accurate (though perhaps overly cynical) to describe a typical student writing process in this way:

   ▷ Receive the assignment from the instructor.
   ▷ Check the due date and other requirements such as word count.
   ▷ Put the assignment away.
   ▷ A day or two before the due date, re-read the assignment.
   ▷ Google the subject of the assignment, and take a few notes.
   ▷ Look for relevant notes from the instructor.
   ▷ Create a new document in a word processor.

▷ Using the notes from the internet search and from class, start writing.

▷ Write an introduction first and then just keep writing until reaching the required word count.

▷ Integrate quotes from the internet search so as to demonstrate that research was conducted.

▷ Spell check and grammar check the document.

▷ Perhaps read it over once and make some minor revisions.

▷ Submit.

Discuss the realities of how you approach writing assignments in comparison with what you've been taught. If your writing process is more similar to that described above than it is to the ideal process outlined earlier in this chapter, do you think the use of GenAI would be more likely to bring you closer to the ideal or more likely to pull you further away from it?

2. This chapter concludes with the metaphor of reaching the top of Mount Everest by climbing or by helicopter. Discuss this metaphor and whether it affects your perspective on writing.

05

PROMPTS

■ LEARNING OBJECTIVES ■

▷ Identify the role of prompts in GenAI usage.
▷ Explain the function of prompt engineering.
▷ Describe the characteristics of an effective prompt.
▷ Recognize effective prompt-revision strategies.
▷ Demonstrate strong prompt-writing skills.

■ BEFORE YOU READ THIS CHAPTER ■

What does it mean to prompt someone? How do instructors use writing prompts to direct students to take on specific writing tasks? What are the differences between an effective prompt for a human writer and an effective prompt for an AI?

INTRODUCTION

The process of writing prompts and subsequently adjusting them is referred to as **prompt engineering**. As with any other tool, getting the results you want from GenAI requires skillful execution—in this case, through successful prompt engineering. Simple prompts are likely to return simple answers, and unclear prompts are likely to return outputs misaligned with your needs. Because weak prompts can translate to weak writing, this chapter focuses on improving your strategies for writing prompts and your understanding of how prompt engineering works.

WRITING EFFECTIVE PROMPTS

Prompts are instructions used to encourage a reaction. For example, one might prompt a hesitant speaker with a simple question in order to get them to start talking. Academic writing assignments are also a type of prompt, intended to lead the student to create a desired output. There are many ways to prompt someone: a few words of encouragement, a suggestive phrase, an inquisitive look, even a gesture. Written prompts often take the form of explicit instructions.

A prompt for GenAI should encourage it to generate the type of output that the user intends. Good prompts are typically

- ▷ **Clear:** Remember that GenAI programs don't interpret meanings in the ways that we do. They cannot make assumptions about what is *really* intended as opposed to what is stated. Thus, clarity is central to effective prompt writing. Ambiguous prompts may leave GenAI programs guessing as to what's intended, and may also increase the likelihood of hallucinations.

- ▷ **Specific:** Prompts need to be specific, so that the GenAI has sufficient details from which to extrapolate an output. Vague prompts can result in vague or generic outputs. For example, asking a GenAI program to "write an essay about *Wuthering Heights*" or "create an article about internet censorship" will not likely result in a strong output.

- ▷ **Contextual:** Prompts that don't provide contextual details are more likely to result in outputs that miss the mark. Provide as many contextual details and as much background information as possible, including the intended audience, the scenario that the writing is for (a piece of journalism, a brief professional email, etc.), and the intended tone and style.

▷ **Accurate:** GenAI programs cannot currently discern between correct and incorrect information. So, if you use inaccurate information as part of your prompt, GenAI will assume your prompt's claims to be true, likely returning an output that itself contains false information. (Incorrect information used in a prompt also becomes part of the GenAI's LLM, which may poison future outputs from that GenAI program as well.)

▷ **Ethical:** Every academic discipline, profession, and personal situation brings with it a set of ethical expectations that should be accounted for. In general, prompts should avoid directing GenAI toward offensive content, intentionally misleading content, and content that might lead to harm. It's important to keep in mind as well that GenAI programs often exhibit biases (see Chapter 9), and prompts should be written with an awareness of these biases.

Provocation

Classroom writing assignments are themselves sometimes referred to as writing prompts. They're meant to encourage you to respond to the assignment in a particular way; they guide toward a desired outcome. However, they're designed to encourage and guide a human student writer, not a GenAI. Compare an effective writing assignment with an effective GenAI prompt aimed at a similar output. Is it wrong for students to revise classroom writing assignments in order to make them more effective prompts for GenAI? Should instructors include advice or even exact language for prompting GenAI when they provide writing assignments to their students?

REFINING PROMPTS

Effective prompts are the result of refinement and nuanced revision. Some refinements may require restructuring of the prompt; others may require only that a word or two be changed. The process of prompt engineering is one of trial and error, and it's difficult to provide general rules for success. Nonetheless, there are some strategies that you should consider when your initial prompts don't lead to the outputs you intend:

- ▷ **Clarify details of the task:** You need to be able to identify exactly what it is you're looking for, including the number of words, the type of sources that you wish to draw on, and the intended audience.

- ▷ **Identify any restrictions:** You should identify any constraints on the task. For example, "avoid the use of first-person language."

- ▷ **Structure and order the prompt:** One method for this is to use a fill-in-the-blank approach. For example, "provide discussion of three key aspects of opportunity cost: 1. _____ 2. _____ 3. _____."

- ▷ **Provide input/output examples:** You can provide GenAI with examples of outputs that illustrate the style or format you wish to receive as an output. For example, you can prompt the GenAI program to "create an output to this prompt that resembles the following: _____."

- ▷ **Use introductory cues (called "prefixes"):** Using specific cues at the beginning of a prompt sentence shows the GenAI the contexts, styles, forms, or other conditions you wish the output to account for. For example, you might write a prompt with the prefix, "in a voice appropriate to a business workplace, write a report ..." or "writing as if you were a biologist, write a ..."

Since prompt engineering is repetitive and iterative, writing prompts for GenAI may seem tedious or laborious; indeed, the process requires significant amounts of work. The difficulty of prompt engineering disrupts the myth that GenAI programs can simply be told what to do with little thought on the part of the human user.

END OF CHAPTER MATERIALS

So What?

1. The norms and ethical values at play in writing often vary depending on academic, professional, and personal context. So what? Should we be willing to use certain prompts in some contexts but not others? For example, would it be acceptable to prompt a GenAI program to draft a work-related email, but unacceptable to prompt it to draft an academic assignment?

2. As discussed above, prompt engineering can be quite difficult. So what does this entail for you? Does it make the use of GenAI less appealing? Is GenAI less effective than you may have initially thought?

Conceptual AI

1. It would be quite unusual for a writing instructor to refine a writing assignment after students submitted their responses so as to obtain answers more in line with the instructor's intentions. That is, instructors don't usually prompt engineer their assignments. Should they? (Note: Instructors *do* often revise assignments for the next time they teach the same course, based on how the previous cohort of students responded.)

2. Garry Trudeau's comic strip *Doonesbury* is known for its clever political and social satire. Trudeau has been publishing the strip for more than fifty years and was the first winner of a Pulitzer Prize for a comic. The strip reprinted below, from May 7th of 2023, is an interesting commentary on the rapid rise of prompt engineering in the workplace, introducing what Trudeau refers to as "AI promptives."

DOONESBURY   **BY GARRY TRUDEAU**

How does Trudeau portray the difference in acceptance of GenAI across age groups? Is Trudeau making fun of the older generation or of the younger generation? What does the strip suggest about GenAI's potential impact on the availability of different careers?

Applied AI

Write a prompt in connection with a writing task you've recently had to perform—this could be a course assignment, a workplace task, or a personal writing project such as an email to a friend or an itinerary for a vacation. Input this prompt into a GenAI program such as ChatGPT and examine the results. Next, refine your prompt one or more times until the GenAI program produces a result that suits your intended purpose or that could serve as an effective starting point for further revision outside of the AI program.

Based on this experience, create a document that teaches beginners how to write and refine GenAI prompts for similar tasks. This chapter serves as a generalized introduction to creating prompts; but now, instead of focusing on general recommendations, try to create instructions that are specific to the type of writing task you've just attempted.

For Discussion

Should colleges and universities develop more formal ways to teach prompt engineering? If prompt engineers are an emerging profession, and if prompt engineering is a skill anyone who uses GenAI will need, are educational institutions obligated to teach it?

06

VISUALS

■ **LEARNING OBJECTIVES** ▬▬▬▬▬▬▬▬▬

▷ Examine the role of visual rhetoric in GenAI.
▷ Describe the uses of GenAI in multimodal writing.
▷ Practice producing visual content.
▷ Understand the role of hallucinations in GenAI-produced visuals.
▷ Apply visuals ethically.

■ **BEFORE YOU READ THIS CHAPTER** ▬▬▬▬▬▬

Think about the role visuals play in writing. Do you include visuals in your own writing? If so, where do you get those images? How do you decide where they go? Do you adjust them to fit your needs? What are the constraints you face when incorporating images?

INTRODUCTION

In March 2023, photographer Boris Eldagsen won the "Creative" category of the Sony World Photography Award for his picture *PSEUDOMNESIA: The Electrician.*

The Sony website described Eldagsen's photo as "a haunting black-and-white portrait of two women from different generations, reminiscent of the visual language of 1940s family portraits."[23] Indeed, it is a stunning image. However, Eldagsen revealed afterward that the "photograph" was in fact created using the GenAI platform Dall-E 2 and that he would decline the award. He explained that he entered this image as a "cheeky monkey," in order to see whether photography competitions are prepared for the introduction of GenAI. "They are not," he concluded.[24]

Eldagsen's experiment encouraged conversations about the role of GenAI in creativity and how GenAI might change what we think of as art. Many professional artists—including designers and graphic artists—see GenAI as a threat to their professions.

Culturally, we've embraced the idea that photographic images accurately represent the world. Clichés such as "photographic evidence" and "pics or it didn't happen" reflect our trust in the photograph. Yet, from the moment we invented photography, we've had the ability to manipulate photographs to suit our interests. And throughout the history of photography there have been countless instances where images initially received as accurate were revealed later to have been manipulated.[25] Photographic editing isn't at all new; however, the introduction of digital imagery in recent decades has made it far easier for anyone—including the layperson—to make adjustments and alterations. Even the default applications on our mobile devices include software for quick changes: cropping, color adjustment, and color filters. Now, GenAI has expanded our ability to manipulate photographs further still.

Current forms of writing are now far more likely to include imagery than at any point in the past. Think of how many combinations of text and imagery—memes, social media pics, videos with captions or overlaid text, and so on—you engage with on a regular basis. In what ways does GenAI bear on the relationship between writing and imagery, and in what ways should we learn to deploy GenAI imagery in our writing?

VISUAL RHETORIC AND GenAI

Visuals—including photographs, videos, symbols, icons, charts, tables, and comics—all provide information. Because they convey information, we can say that these visual elements are rhetorical, and that how we choose to use them is a rhetorical decision. **Visual rhetoric** refers to the ways in which we use visuals to communicate information and meaning to our readers.

We all make choices about how to obtain and integrate visuals. When you chose to post one selfie rather than another, you're making a rhetorical choice. Even our small typographical decisions—such as whether to use **bold**, *italics*, a specific font, or a specific placement on the page or screen—affect how our readers receive and interpret the information we convey. Visuals can be used to increase readers' comprehension, to clarify information, illustrate details or examples, gain readers' attention, highlight key information, establish authority, and tailor our communications to different audiences.

Traditionally, writers have had three ways of obtaining visuals:

1. **Finding:** Locating visuals that someone else has already made and repurposing them (obtaining permission to do so if needed).

2. **Commissioning:** Arranging for visuals to be created by someone else so as to suit the writer's purpose.

3. **Making:** This can include such things as taking original photographs, creating new artwork, or developing appropriate charts and diagrams.

We now have a fourth option:

4. **GenAI outputs:** GenAI can create visual content that aligns with a writer's specific objectives. This can include realistic photograph-style images, diagrams, and even more abstract artwork portraying visual metaphors or symbolism.

In addition to image generation, GenAI also allows users to work with visuals in a variety of other ways. It is rapidly becoming an effective tool for

▷ **Data analysis:** GenAI can be used to analyze and interpret large visual datasets. It can identify patterns, trends, differences, and similarities and suggest ways in which visual elements can be effectively integrated. This information can be useful from an analytical perspective, as it can help writers and designers to better understand how to adjust their own uses of visuals in ways that are rhetorically effective. For example, GenAI can be asked to examine popular styles in online advertising so as to identify which techniques best attract readers' attention. It can then be asked to design a new advertisement in a similar style. Even if this new output isn't suitable as a final product, it may offer inspiration for a professional design informed by trends the AI has identified.

▷ **Data visualization:** This is the practice of representing data and information in visual forms—such as charts, tables, and infographics—in order to facilitate analysis, comprehension, and effective communication. GenAI can be prompted to create dynamic visuals that convey a complex set of data in an accessible way.

▷ **Experimentation:** Many visual GenAI platforms provide multiple outputs to a single prompt. For example, Dall-E 2 was prompted to generate "a photographic quality image of a shark wearing a space helmet," and it returned the four options pictured below.[26] In this way, GenAI can help inspire writers, designers, and artists by providing multiple approaches for comparison.

▷ **Customization:** GenAI can be used to tailor existing visual material to specific audiences or to specific authorial needs. Many image editing platforms now offer internalized GenAI tools that can generate or revise visual content. For example, Adobe's "Generative Fill" tool can create new parts of an image that didn't appear in the original, or remove content seamlessly and instantly. Suppose, for example, that you took a photograph of the mountains of Denali National

Provocation

The 1938 photograph below is identified as "Salmon fishing with large loop nets by Native Americans. Tribal tradition determines the spot each tribal member fishes from." It was made using standard camera equipment available in the 1930s. Suppose we were to use an AI tool such as Adobe's "Generative Fill" to extend this image further to the left and right, beyond what's available in the photograph. The additional content in the photo would be completely artificial. Does the ability to extend visuals such as this affect our understanding of the image? Is it acceptable to make such revisions to a historical image? Does this depend on the subject of the image—such as whether it includes real people or cultural groups?

Park, using an iPhone's standard 4:3 aspect ratio. You could then use Generative Fill to extend that photograph to a wider format such as 16:9 if this format was more appropriate to the medium in which you wished to use the image. The Generative Fill tool would extend the image beyond its original frame, filling in the left and right of the original with a prediction of what *could* be in that visual space, in much the same way that ChatGPT predicts what *could* be the next word in a sentence.

FROM WORDS TO IMAGES

Making visuals with GenAI requires creative and detailed thinking about what you want the visual to be and, importantly, how that translates into a prompt. Prompts for visuals need to be quite specific. Unlike an online search engine, which can locate pre-existing images using only a minimal prompt, GenAI requires thorough guidance. The following strategies can be useful in designing effective visual prompts:

1. **Be specific and clear:** The more specific the prompt, the more likely the GenAI will return outputs that meet your needs. Vague or ambiguous prompts will make the GenAI more likely focus on patterns entrenched in the LLM instead of an image tailored to your specific needs. Instead of saying that you want "a factory," use an adjective–noun paring to provide more details: "dilapidated factory," "brick-built factory," or "abandoned factory." Rather than simply writing that you want an image of "a dog," specify its desired species, color, actions, and other relevant details. Visual GenAI programs often work well with descriptive and metaphorical language, so don't shy away from this. For example: "A golden retriever jumping to catch a ball; the fur of the dog resembles an almond dipped in honey."[27]

2. **Provide examples:** Providing the GenAI with a few examples of other visuals can help it to better understand what you're looking for. In many image generators, you can provide examples by either referring to specific (famous) images in the prompt or by including links to those images. You can also use examples to specify details or traits you wish the GenAI to replicate, such as artistic styles, colors, or patterns.

3. **Explain the context:** When provided with contextual details, GenAI can create an image that better fits with the tone you wish to achieve. Don't try to cram all of these details into a single sentence; instead, write multi-sentence prompts. For example, if you need an image of the open ocean, instead of a short generic prompt such  as "the open ocean," use one with greater contextual information: "The open ocean early in the morning just as the sun rises on the horizon. There are a few rain clouds in the background. Two gulls fly by. The air is clear with no haze."[28]

4. **Describe the intended tone:** Often, the objective in using visuals in a piece of writing is to connect with the audience. You may wish to trigger the audience to *feel* a particular way through the visual. Using emotional terms in a prompt helps the GenAI create a visual with more appropriate tone. Compare these two images, one (left) generated by a prompt for "a dilapidated factory, conveying a nostalgic sensation" and the other (right) generated by a prompt for "a dilapidated factory, conveying a feeling of palpable tension."[29]

5. **Revise and regenerate:** As with all writing, revision is critical. Most GenAI image generators will produce several possible outcomes when you provide a prompt. They also usually include a button to "regenerate" images from the same prompt, giving you still more options. If the output of your first prompt isn't quite what you're looking for, revise the prompt to specifically clarify the desired changes. Experimenting with multiple prompts and trying different revisions may lead to unexpectedly dynamic outputs.

VISUALS AND HALLUCINATIONS

GenAI visuals are highly susceptible to hallucinations (as discussed in Chapter 2). Sometimes, recognizing a visual hallucination is easy. For example, GenAI often has difficulty rendering human hands:[30]

Other times, however, visual hallucinations are less obvious. Here are some strategies for identifying visual hallucinations:

▷ **Understand real-world images:** By familiarizing yourself with other images of your intended subject, you'll be better prepared to identify errors in the GenAI output. For example, if you ask a GenAI to create an image of a building in the style of Victorian architecture, you should study other real-world images of Victorian architecture, comparing their style and characteristics against the GenAI output. This will allow you to identify obviously out-of-place, implausible, or incorrect elements.

▷ **Confirm the wording:** Check to be sure that the prompt you provided is understood by the GenAI program as you intend. Sometimes GenAI may combine or misinterpret the different elements of a long or complex prompt. This is also why short, direct sentences can be most effective in a prompt.

▷ **Review for stylistic consistency:** Make sure the style of the visual output is consistent. For example, if you've prompted a GenAI to generate a photographic image of a long-distance runner, and it returns an image that is mostly photographic but in which the background crowd looks like a painting, you'll likely need to revise.

▷ **Seek feedback:** Just as you should seek reader input when revising a written document, you should ask someone else to review images you've created using GenAI. Remember, using GenAI is part of human–machine collaboration. Involving another human reviewer enhances that collaboration and ensures human oversight of the process.

VISUALS AND ETHICS

As with AI-generated writing, there are concerns related to integrity and ethics that go along with how and when you integrate GenAI visuals into your writing. First and foremost, as argued in Chapter 3, *transparency* and *documentation* are crucial to the ethical use of GenAI visuals. You should always indicate when a visual has been created by GenAI. Likewise, there are several other ethical considerations to keep in mind:

▷ **Manipulation:** GenAI offers you the opportunity to change images to suit your purpose. However, manipulated visuals can be used to present false or misleading information. **Deep fakes** are images of particular people—typically celebrities and politicians but potentially also private individuals—that appear convincingly real, and which often show their subject doing something unflattering or uncharacteristic. These images can be used to harm a person's reputation or even humiliate them. They can also misinform and alter opinions on the basis of false information. Such usage is clearly unethical and it violates the standards of integrity and transparency that we should all abide by.

▷ **Concealment:** Visuals can conceal information. For example, an image of the effects of an oil spill on a coastline could be cropped so as not to show all parts of the affected area. GenAI technologies can even be used to generatively replace images of damaged areas with pristine representations, thus concealing the actual damage.

▷ **Replacement of human labor:** As noted earlier, an important traditional way of obtaining visuals is through the commissioning of artwork and designs. When considering the use of GenAI to produce visuals, consider any implications this may have on the livelihood of artists that may otherwise be employed to create those visuals.

END OF CHAPTER MATERIALS

So What?

1. In March 2023, Coca Cola released a commercial titled "Coca-Cola Masterpiece,"[31] which was generated by AI Studios, a text-to-video AI platform. So what? Does it matter, ethically or practically, whether people make videos and films using GenAI rather than traditional actors and animators?

Conceptual AI

1. Will the ability to generate specialized visuals using GenAI programs affect how and when you incorporate visuals into your writing?

2. How might we as readers need to adjust the ways in which we engage with visual information, given the use of GenAI and the potential for hallucinations?

3. To better understand the relationship between description and GenAI prompt-writing, locate a paragraph of particularly descriptive writing, perhaps from a favorite book or from an interesting article you've recently read. The paragraph may provide details about a character, a setting, a person, an event, or an idea. Use some or all of that description as a prompt for an AI image generator, asking it to create a picture of what's described. Does the output match what you initially had in mind after reading the description? How might you refine the prompt to better fit with what you pictured?

Applied AI

1. Using a GenAI image generator, write a prompt to produce a photo-graph-quality image that represents one of the following: the landscape of one of your favorite places, a particular animal, or a well-known his-torical event. How accurate is the GenAI's output? Compare it against "real" images of the subject in your prompt.

2. There are hundreds of video tutorials online teaching how to make incredible GenAI images. Locate one such tutorial on YouTube, TikTok, or any other platform, and watch it. Next, use the information in that video to create an image. Did the resulting image match your expecta-tions? Why or why not?

3. Think of a piece of writing you've recently composed that might ben-efit from the addition of an image. Write a prompt to generate that image. Then, revise the prompt multiple times until you get an output you're satisfied with. For each revision of the prompt, copy and paste the prompt text and the GenAI's output into a separate document, con-structing a chronology of your revisions and the corresponding out-puts. Analyze the progression of your prompt writing and the outputs, and explain how you transitioned from the first iteration of the prompt to the next based on the output at each step.

For Discussion

1. After announcing that *PSEUDOMNESIA: The Electrician* was created using Dall-E2, Boris Eldagsen was interviewed by media outlets around the world. One of the more widely circulated interviews was published by *Scientific American.*[32] Read the *Scientific American* interview and dis-cuss Eldagsen's comments about GenAI. Does his perspective change your opinion on whether GenAI has a role in the art world?

2. Getting GenAI to return visuals that are effective and aesthetically pleasing requires careful and detailed prompts. This leads to a rather different first step in the process of creating a visual work: instead of conceiving of an image visually in one's mind, it's necessary to clearly articulate the image in writing. Discuss the ways in which this new approach may bear on the creativity involved in making visuals.

07

CONTEXTS OF USE

▷ Identify the value and risks associated with GenAI in various contexts.
▷ Examine the potential uses of Gen AI in academic, professional, civic, and personal contexts.
▷ Recognize the importance of integrity when using GenAI in each context.

■ BEFORE YOU READ THIS CHAPTER ▮▮▮▮▮▮▮▮▮▮▮▮▮▮▮▮▮▮▮▮▮

Think about the different kinds of writing you will probably have to produce in your career, in your civic life, and in your personal life. Make a list of those possible tasks and of the ways in which GenAI might be a valuable collaborator for completing them.

INTRODUCTION

You've probably heard the old real estate adage, "location, location, location," which implies that the value of a piece of property is primarily about where it's located. We can adopt a similar axiom toward GenAI: context, context, context. *How* you should use GenAI has a lot to do with the context in which you're using it. For example, how you use GenAI in your academic work will probably be different from how you use it in professional contexts such as a job or internship; how you use it in civic/political writing, or in personal writing, will differ again. This chapter explores the application of GenAI in those four distinct writing contexts: academic, professional, civic, and personal.

ACADEMIC CONTEXTS

There's an increasing belief that college and university students need to learn and practice the forms of writing they're more likely to produce in their careers. Some academic disciplines design their curricula specifically around the relationships between industry and education. Industry standards change (frequently because of technological changes, as we're witnessing with AI), so educational institutions that target job-specific skills must react and revise their curricula often. Higher education so heavily emphasizes writing and communication in part because nearly every industry now identifies communication skills—written, visual, and spoken—as primary qualifications when hiring new employees. These also happen to be areas in which GenAI is having significant impact.

Traditionally, the primary assignment in academic writing has been the essay. First-year writing programs often focus on essay writing simply because those programs are designed to prepare students for further courses, many of which will themselves require essays. However, it's unlikely—though not impossible—that you will ever be asked to write an essay after finishing college. For this reason, many instructors now assign writing forms other than essays. The rise of digital media has drastically altered the kinds of writing we produce, and has increased the role of visuals used in conjunction with writing.

GenAI can be a useful tool for forms of writing, from essays and multimodal writing to visual rhetoric and even programming:

▷ Text generators and editors such as ChatGPT, Grammarly, Jasper, Wordtune, AnyWord, and QuillBot can help with generating, revising, and editing text, whether for use in an essay or in some other form of writing.

▷ Visual GenAI programs such as Dall-E, MidJourney, Firefly, and Express can generate original images.

▷ Conventional image programs such as Photoshop use integrated GenAI tools for editing and revising images.

▷ InVideo, Synthesia, Pictory, and Veed.io can be useful for generating and editing film.

▷ Aviva, Soundful, Boomy, Loudly, and Soundraw can produce original music.

▷ Platforms like TabNine, Codex, CodeWP, and CodeSquire can assist in writing computer code.

In all academic writing contexts, be sure to adhere to your college's or university's policies regarding GenAI, as well as your instructor's course-specific policies.

Provocation

Many people claim that they can reliably identify work written by GenAI because, it's said, the language doesn't "sound" like that of a real person—it's flat and repetitive. But if this is true, is the flat voice of the GenAI partly a result of the text being presented on a page or screen, rather than orally?

Try this: prompt a GenAI to write two paragraphs about any subject you choose. Don't revise the text. Practice reading the content out loud until you are familiar and comfortable with it. Then, deliver it like a speech to someone else. Can your audience discern whether it's GenAI-generated?

Next, try using a text-to-speech AI such as Speechify or Revoicer to read the text in a computer-generated voice. How does that delivery of the content compare to your own reading?

PROFESSIONAL CONTEXTS

According to the World Economic Forum's (WEF's) *Future of Jobs Report 2023*, the category of job that's expected to grow the fastest over the next few years is "AI and Machine Learning Specialist."[33] The WEF also reports that the proportion of labor tasked to machines instead of humans is rapidly increasing.

ESTIMATED PROPORTION OF TASKS COMPLETED BY HUMANS VS. MACHINES[34]

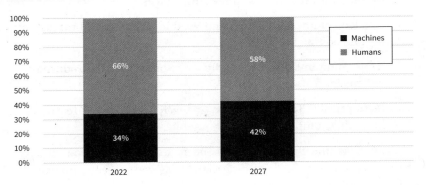

However, this change in the division of labor doesn't necessarily mean that there will be a net reduction in human jobs, at least not in all fields. Aside from the fear of widespread academic cheating, arguably the biggest panic arising with the public emergence of GenAI has been with regard to job loss. And while it's true, according to the WEF's predictions, that many people will be displaced from their jobs by GenAI, it's also expected that even more jobs will be *created* by GenAI:

EXPECTED IMPACT OF TECHNOLOGY ON JOBS, 2023–27[35]

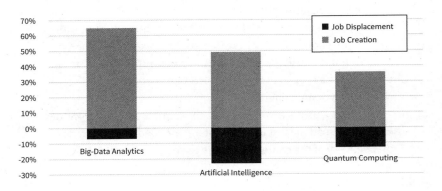

Understanding how to deploy AI and GenAI in professional contexts will be a critical part of most of our professional lives.

Part of the difference between academic writing and workplace writing is that in the workplace the "show your work" demonstration is rarely important, and likely never requested. *The outcome is the important part.* Your colleagues, co-workers, supervisors, and superiors are probably not interested in knowing how many drafts you wrote, or how much you revised in order to get to the final product. They just want to see that the final product is complete and successful. In this way, one of the major disadvantages of GenAI in academic contexts—the fact that it often functions as a kind of black box and doesn't reveal its process in producing an output—is far less of a hindrance in professional contexts.

In many workplaces, GenAI is already now commonly deployed to assist with a wide range of writing tasks, including writing emails, responding to customer inquiries, sending automated responses, setting internal reminders, drafting news releases, summarizing correspondence, creating reports, producing technical manuals, and drafting proposals. Collaborating with GenAI to complete these tasks can lead to greatly increased productivity, as well as improved quality and accuracy.

Consider in greater detail some of the ways in which GenAI can assist in these contexts:

▷ **Cover letters:** In most professions, applying for a job requires that you submit a cover letter, which generally includes information such as where you first learned about the job (an ad, a personal referral, etc.), a summary of your work experience, skills that are pertinent to the job, and contact information. There are many GenAI tools that can help with the creation of cover letters. Even conventional word processors such as Microsoft Word include cover letter templates that provide GenAI-driven suggestions for wording and formatting. GenAI can help you structure a cover letter to be more dynamic; it can also help you customize your letter for the specific job and company, and revise it to best represent your abilities in ways that will attract the attention of potential employers. You can also converse with GenAI to identify the key assets that employees in similar positions need and the challenges they typically face. GenAI can also be prompted to shape a cover letter to fit within a given word count, cutting out repetition and focusing on the most important elements of your skill set and background.

▷ **Résumés:** It may seem most efficient to simply provide GenAI with all the data that should be included in your résumé and then prompt it to generate an output based on that data. However, doing so will likely result in a bland, generic résumé. To obtain an effective result, you may need to provide multiple prompts. Suppose you begin by prompting the GenAI to identify the most important qualifications of the job for which you are applying. You can then prompt it to customize your résumé to emphasize the ways in which your background and skillset matches with the job's qualifications. Remember, however, that the GenAI may hallucinate qualifications and experiences you don't have in order to fulfill the demands of the prompt, so be sure to carefully check the output for any false information.

▷ **Onboarding reports:** Many companies appreciate when new employees provide an overview as to how they can most effectively integrate into the workplace. Onboarding reports allow new employees to describe their strengths and make suggestions for how to maximally utilize those strengths in a new job. GenAI programs can be particularly helpful here, as they can effectively fit a summary of your experiences and aspirations into the metrics and requirements of an onboarding report. Many GenAI platforms can also be prompted to adapt such information into table or spreadsheet formats, so as to produce the types of schedules and performance plans that are often requested alongside written onboarding reports. For example, you could prompt a GenAI to examine your report and generate a table showing what you wish to accomplish in 30 days, 60 days, 90 days, and so on.

▷ **Project briefs and reports:** Project briefs and reports typically describe the objectives, purposes, outputs, audiences, timelines, budgets, member assignments, expectations, and other pertinent details of major work projects. Writing these can be tedious because of the many different types of information that need to be included. However, by providing a GenAI with each component part of the relevant data, you can often produce a working draft that will serve as a strong starting point for further revision. GenAI can also adapt its output to meet specific formatting requirements such as a company's report template. In the absence of a template, it can be useful in suggesting organizational approaches and identifying missing elements.

▷ **Feedback analyses:** Feedback analyses are documents that analyze feedback information—such as customer reviews—and synthesize that data into a manageable and interpretable form. This might include quantitative data, such as customer satisfaction surveys: "How likely is it, from 1 to 5, that you would recommend this product to a friend?" Or it might be written evaluations: "Please describe your experience with our customer service team." GenAI can assist in analyzing and synthesizing such information into a more useful format. For example, it can categorize data if you provide it with the intended criteria: "organize these written responses from those that are most positive to those that are most negative." If prompted in this way, the AI can scrub the provided data for words and expressions frequently used in positive responses, such as "good," "appreciated," "will recommend," and so on. This can be enormously helpful if you're trying to identify the features of a product or service that are going well, or if you're trying to identify the problems. GenAI can also help organize feedback data into reports or executive summaries, and can identify repeated bits of feedback that may be useful for developing actionable insights or responses from the data.

▷ **Collaborative writing:** Workplace writing is often collaborative. We all have differences in our writing and communication styles, and GenAI can be a useful tool for synthesizing the collaborative parts of different peoples' writing into a single cohesive document. It can revise supplied text into a single document with a consistent tone, style, format, and approach.

▷ **Presentations:** Whether internally (for other employees or supervisors) or externally (for customers, investors, or other public audiences), it's likely that at some point in your career you will have to make a presentation. GenAI can help in organizing your information in a way that will make sense to your audience. It can also help you to fine-tune your language to best connect with a specific audience (be sure to mention your audience in your prompt to the AI), and it can even provide advice about how to make your presentation more dynamic and engaging.

▷ **Graphics and visuals:** Some companies employ graphic artists and designers to make and design visual assets for company documents. However, not all companies have the resources for this, and often employees are expected to provide visual information to accompany their written documentation. GenAI can help produce and edit all kinds of visual content, ranging from charts and tables to infographics, diagrams, schematics, and even photograph-quality images and video. In some cases, this content can be produced by simply providing the GenAI with the accompanying written documentation and prompting it to create an accompanying chart (or diagram, etc.).

These are only a few examples of the many kinds of workplace writing that you may be required to produce in your career, and there are many additional ways to collaborate with GenAI to complete these and other writing tasks.

Keep in mind that, as in academic settings, professional contexts often have specific approaches to integrity. Be sure to understand your company's policies about GenAI, and don't run afoul of company or industry practices.

CIVIC CONTEXTS

In addition to your academic career and your professional career, you may also find moments in your life when you need to write about civic issues for public audiences. This kind of writing is often described as political, even when the objective—such as asking for volunteers to help clean up a local park—isn't "political" in the usual sense. Civic writing is vital to our social and democratic processes.

Civics educator Sandra Stotsky identifies civic writing as including "formal legal writing [such] as speeches, petitions, and resolutions ... formal organizational writing [such] as minutes of meetings, agendas, memos, and newsletters ... and informal and personal writing, such as letters to friends, relatives, or neighbors supporting or opposing candidates for public office."[36] Stotsky also identifies five major purposes for civic writing: "[1] to personalize civic relationships with public officials and/or to express a civic identity with other citizens ... [2] to obtain information or assistance ... [3] to provide public information or to offer a public service ... [4] to evaluate public officials or services ... [and 5] to advocate for people or causes."[37]

GenAI can be useful in crafting not only long-form civic writing such as political speeches, but also social media posts and interactions. Social media is now central to all kinds of civic writing, as is evident from the role it plays in politics, from presidential candidates' Twitter feeds to citizen reporting at rallies. While some impromptu social media posts may not involve the degree of careful composition typical of writing in academic and professional contexts, it is writing all the same.

Because social media is public and often meant to persuade an audience, replies and interactions are often argumentative or even adversarial. GenAI can be particularly helpful in crafting responses to reactive or aggressive people. One can prompt a GenAI program to quickly produce measured and adaptive responses that fit appropriately in response to hostile or argumentative social media interactions.

GenAI can also be useful in providing predictive suggestions for the most effective language to use for persuasion in given conversational exchange. It can even help you analyze others' responses so as to better understand their arguments and interests, rapidly creating more effective and individualized responses than may be possible otherwise.

Civic writing demands particular attention to the risk of AI hallucinations. Including inaccurate or obfuscating information in civic writing—especially in social media—can result in people reacting negatively, or even dismissing your credibility. In the realm of politics, your credibility—your *ethos*—is crucial to how readers respond.

PERSONAL CONTEXTS

Often, courses in academic writing begin with personal writing—usually in the form of a personal essay—so as to encourage students to focus on the act of writing rather than the content. The key element of personal writing is how you chose to represent your thoughts—that is, your voice.

One of the things that GenAI isn't (yet) good at is writing in a specific person's voice. GenAI doesn't know your ideas, values, or thinking processes. Thus, simply asking GenAI to produce a piece of personal writing in your voice is likely to lead to a poor or generic result.

That said, there are three ways in which GenAI might assist you with personal writing:

1. It can help you generate ideas. Suppose you recently visited another country that you'd never seen before. During that visit, you recognized some cultural differences between the other country and your home. These differences intrigue you, and you decide to write a personal essay expressing your observations and thoughts, which you wish to submit to a school publication or a travel blog. If you simply prompt

a GenAI program to "write a personal essay about the cultural differences between *this other country* and *your home country*," it might successfully identify some genuine distinctions; but none would be from your perspective, and the writing will fail to capture your authorial voice. The output wouldn't be at all appropriate as a personal essay. *However*, what it might do is point toward some specific difference that hadn't previously occurred to you, which can then be incorporated into your thinking and writing about your travels and observations.

2. GenAI can help you revise your writing into language that will be clear and readable for public audiences. Because personal writing often deeply connects with the writer's own thoughts, it's not uncommon for it to make perfect sense to the writer while being far less clear to any other reader. GenAI can be used to identify whether a piece of writing is clearly expressed, and to make suggestions for revision that will improve clarity and eliminate ambiguities.

3. GenAI can help you make connections between distinct ideas in order to create a more cohesive piece of writing. For example, you can prompt a GenAI with a series of thoughts you have on a particular topic, asking it to describe the possible interconnections between those thoughts and the best order in which to coherently articulate them. Cohesion will assist your audience in understanding the point you wish to convey.

Ultimately, any personal writing you produce should reflect your own thoughts and ideas. Since personal writing is meant to be a reflection of you as writer, GenAI shouldn't be used in ways that lead your writing to be anything other than a sincere expression of your values.

END OF CHAPTER MATERIALS

So What?

1. The conventions and the purposes of writing vary greatly among the four contexts addressed in this chapter. So what? Is it better to adapt our writing to each context, or is consistency more important?

2. The use of GenAI brings with it certain risks, and these risks can be greater in some contexts than in others. So what does that matter?

Should we feel more comfortable using GenAI in some of these contexts than in others?

Conceptual AI

How, specifically, is GenAI being used in the field you are studying or in
your career? Conduct some research: speak with practitioners in your
field, consider the various types of writing they typically do, and examine
any relevant GenAI programs. How widespread is the use of GenAI in your
field, and has it proved to be helpful or harmful?

Applied AI

1. Reaction videos display someone's reaction to a first encounter with
   something—such as the first time they see a movie or hear a song.
   Prompt a GenAI to write a personal essay about something meaningful
   to you that you'd like to share with others. This may be an essay about
   your favorite movie series, favorite book, favorite YouTuber, a hobby,
   or anything else you enjoy. Or it may be about something you dislike:
   a personal essay about a political situation, a current trend, a public
   figure, or another topic that you feel passionate about.

   Don't immediately read the GenAI's output. Instead, turn on your
   computer or phone's camera and press "record." Read the output
   while recording yourself, creating a reaction video of you reading the
   GenAI's personal essay. Then save the recording and watch it. What
   do your reactions tell you about the GenAI's ability to write a personal
   essay on a topic you care about?

2. Choose one of the four contexts discussed in this chapter—academic,
   professional, civic, or personal—and pick a topic falling under that
   heading that you find interesting (for example, "urban planning in
   Houston" as a civic topic, or "business trends in automotive manufacturing" as a professional topic). Prompt a GenAI program to produce a
   500-word essay about that topic in the style of a TED talk. Then, once
   you have the output, revise it and deliver it by making a video, again in
   a TED talk style. How well-suited is the GenAI's essay to this purpose?
   Does the essay make interesting and insightful points? Is it repetitive?
   Is the language engaging?

3. This chapter describes some methods for using GenAI to write dynamic résumés and cover letters. Create a résumé and a cover letter for a job you might consider pursuing.

For Discussion

1. Discuss as a group how you think you might use GenAI in each of the contexts discussed in this chapter—academic, professional, civic, and personal—and what you see as the advantages and drawbacks in doing so.

2. This book doesn't teach the specifics of how to use particular GenAI platforms such as ChatGPT. This is in part because the relevant platforms and techniques change so rapidly that specific instruction becomes quickly dated, and also because the actual use of GenAI varies greatly by discipline and context. So how *should* students learn to use these tools? How do professionals in the workplace learn to use them? Discuss this as a group.

08

CAREER READINESS

▓ LEARNING OBJECTIVES ▓▓▓▓▓▓▓▓▓▓▓▓▓▓▓▓▓▓▓▓▓▓▓▓▓▓▓

▷ Appreciate the role of GenAI in the global economy.
▷ Describe the connection between education and career readiness.
▷ Identify the skills needed to work in GenAI-related careers.
▷ Understand how GenAI may be used to enhance a variety of employment skills.

▓ BEFORE YOU READ THIS CHAPTER ▓▓▓▓▓▓▓▓▓▓▓▓▓▓▓▓▓▓▓▓

How do you think GenAI will affect your career path? As you learn more about GenAI and use it more, do you see ways in which it might benefit your career? Do you see ways in which it might harm your career? How might the work you do with GenAI in college affect what you do after college?

INTRODUCTION

There's no question that AI is changing the employment landscape. It's estimated that by 2030, AI will have increased the global Gross Domestic Product (GDP) by about 26 per cent, or roughly $15.7 trillion[38]—more than the current GDPs of Japan, India, Germany, and the United Kingdom combined.

There are many who worry that the increase in AI use will cause significant job loss. The World Economic Forum (WEF) predicts that although AI will indeed automate many tasks, and thus cause the loss of some jobs, it will also lead to the creation of many other jobs. According to the WEF, some of the biggest positive changes in employment will occur in areas relating to AI, data analysis, and robot engineering.

NEW AND LOST JOBS AS A FRACTION OF CURRENT EMPLOYMENT (2023–27)[39]

Highest Projected Net Growth	*Highest Projected Net Decline*
1. AI and Machine Learning Specialists	1. Bank Tellers and Related Clerks
2. Sustainability Specialists	2. Postal Service Clerks
3. Business Intelligence Analysts	3. Cashiers and Ticket Clerks
4. Information Security Analysts	4. Data Entry Clerks
5. FinTech Engineers	5. Administrative and Executive Secretaries
6. Data Analysts and Scientists	6. Material-Recording and Stock-Keeping Clerks
7. Robot Engineers	7. Accounting, Bookkeeping, and Payroll Clerks
8. Big Data Specialists	8. Home Appliance Installers and Repairers
9. Agricultural Equipment Operators	9. Legislators and Officials
10. Digital Transformation Specialists	10. Statistical, Finance, and Insurance Clerks

While the term 'AI Readiness' is often used in reference to an industry or business's preparedness for the integration of AI, we can think of **AI Literacy** as the skillset that an individual possesses for entering an AI-integrated workforce. AI Literacy is a subset of digital literacy, and an integral part of higher education.

One of the core objectives of higher education is the preparation of students for successful career placement. This chapter examines a handful of the AI Literacy skills that can best prepare students for the workforce.

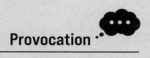

Provocation

Introducing GenAI into existing workflows requires cultural and organizational changes. How radical should this change be? Think of a company operating in an industry that interests you. How would you recommend such a company integrate GenAI into their workplace? How much of this change should come from new hires, as opposed to retraining of an existing workforce?

SKILLS FOR DEVELOPING AND APPLYING GenAI

As noted earlier, the WEF predicts that "AI and Machine Learning Specialists" will be among the most substantial fields of job growth through 2027. There are also many other areas of growth that will almost certainly involve intensive use of GenAI—such as jobs in programming, analytics, and technical support. In any of these contexts, several technical skills are of specific value:

▷ **Prompt engineering:** A strong understanding of prompt engineering is itself a marketable skill (see Chapter 5, and especially the *Doonesbury* comic on page 69).

▷ **Machine learning (ML):** Understanding machine learning concepts and techniques is vital for a career in GenAI. This includes understanding the ways in which GenAI is trained and how its learning algorithms can be improved.

▷ **Natural language processing:** When working with GenAI in language generation or text-to-speech synthesis, it's essential to know how computers process natural language—that is, how they interpret written or spoken human sentences. This is an interdisciplinary area of study and training that includes a mix of computing science and linguistics.

▷ **Data analysis:** With the increasing importance of data-driven decision-making, skills in data analysis, data manipulation, and data visualization are in high demand generally, and are especially useful in GenAI operations.

▷ **Information security:** Understanding the basics of information security is important in order to protect data and maintain privacy. Most employers now expect that new hires will have at least a rudimentary awareness of common security threats as well as best practices for secure data handling, password management, and data encryption. Privacy and security are of particular concern when using GenAI, and employers looking to work with GenAI will almost certainly require that their technical staff have expertise in these areas.

There are countless other technical skills that may be expected depending upon one's profession. Skills in coding, cloud computing, user experience testing, computational modeling, algorithmic thinking, and data manipulation are also greatly valuable to anyone whose career involves the development or application of GenAI.

SKILLS THAT BENEFIT FROM GenAI

Of course, the majority of people aren't likely to work directly in AI development and application. However, there are a great many other career paths for which proficiency in the application of GenAI is likely to be important. According to the WEF,

> ... AI and big data ... is the number three priority in company training strategies from now until 2027, and the number one priority for companies with more than 50,000 employees.... Among technology skills, the ability to efficiently use AI tools now exceeds computer programming by humans, networks and cybersecurity skills, general technological literacy skills, and design and user experience by some margin. In the next five years, AI and big data will comprise more than 40% of the technology training programmes undertaken in surveyed companies operating in the United States, China, Brazil and Indonesia.[40]

The following skills are important to career readiness in nearly any profession, and may importantly benefit from the application of GenAI literacies.

▷ **Basic mathematics and computation:** Many employees are expected to have at least a rudimentary understanding of mathematics and computation. This can include knowing calculus, statistics, and coding. These skills can benefit greatly from the use of GenAI, especially among people who use these skills only intermittently or who aren't naturally gifted in them. For example, GenAI can be effective in drafting and revising computer code; it can also offer guidance in how best to interpret a set of statistical data. Basic knowledge of GenAI prompt engineering can serve to enhance these technical skills in many careers.

▷ **Problem-solving and critical thinking:** Strong problem-solving and critical thinking skills are necessary in order to tackle the complex challenges of any workplace. You should be able to analyze problems, devise creative solutions, and evaluate the performance of competing models. GenAI can be useful here too, as it's an ideal tool for testing hypotheses and running simulations. When prompted appropriately, many GenAI programs are also quite effective in offering innovative solutions to problems or sober and well-considered pro-and-con lists.

▷ **Research skills:** Employees in many fields must be able to navigate research and should understand how best to stay up-to-date with the latest advances in their industries. GenAI applications that analyze, catalog, and synthesize research can be enormously helpful here, especially since time constraints are often a barrier that prevents people from staying up-to-date.

▷ **Communication skills:** Being able to clearly and effectively communicate information and details is critical to nearly all career paths, whether one is communicating externally with customers or internally with colleagues. As discussed throughout this book, GenAI can be enormously helpful as a collaborator in all forms of communications—including written, oral, and visual. Likewise, a strong foundation in written communication is essential to the effective use of GenAI, given the need to write clear and detailed prompts in order to produce effective outputs.

▷ **Initiative and self-motivation:** Employers value employees who demonstrate proactivity, who take initiative, and who show a strong work ethic. One way to demonstrate initiative is to keep abreast of emerging technologies such as GenAI, and to both demonstrate an ability to use those technologies ahead of others and show how using those technologies can be beneficial within one's field of work.

▷ **Time management:** GenAI can be a valuable tool for time management. It can help you divide up your workday and workweek appropriately, and it can also help you create a balanced timeline and schedule for long- and short-term projects. GenAI can also be useful in generating progress reports and updates, ultimately saving time otherwise spent on administrative work and helping you and your co-workers efficiently meet deadlines.

END OF CHAPTER MATERIALS

So What?

1. Does your institution provide opportunities to become career ready through the learning of GenAI skills? So what if they don't? Can you effectively learn these skills independently?

2. Many organizations and industries anticipate that skills with GenAI will be important to their workforce going forward. So what? What might happen if you ignore the emergence of GenAI in your field?

Conceptual AI

1. How is the emergence of GenAI changing your desired profession? Are those changes for the better, in your opinion? Why or why not?

2. How are practitioners of your chosen profession implementing AI skills? From what you can tell, are many people in this profession actively expanding their skillsets to include GenAI? If not, does this present unique opportunities for new employees to offer valuable expertise?

Applied AI

1. Use a GenAI platform to develop a formal report on the status of a profession that interests you. Provide several sections in this report, including

▷   an executive summary
▷   an analysis of current industry trends
▷   skills and areas of expertise needed among the workforce
▷   recommendations for industry change and adaptation

Present this information in a variety of formats: written text, bulleted or numbered lists, infographics, visuals, etc. Were the GenAI's contributions helpful? Were they more helpful in the development of some sections than others?

2. Use a GenAI platform to develop a brief informational document explaining how GenAI is currently being deployed in your chosen profession. Discuss the potential risks and benefits of GenAI to that profession.

For Discussion

1. How has your institution addressed career readiness in terms of GenAI? Identify any areas of skills training that you wish the institution would more effectively provide.

2. Should AI skills be taught as their own topic (perhaps even as a separate post-secondary course), or should they be integrated in the training of other discipline-specific skills (for example, "AI for coding" in computing programs, "AI for critical thinking" in philosophy programs, etc.)? Discuss the ways in which GenAI skills are discipline-specific and the ways in which they're universal.

PART III

Challenges

BIAS

09

■ LEARNING OBJECTIVES

▷ Describe the typical occurrences of bias in GenAI.
▷ Explain algorithmic bias.
▷ Identify multiple forms of exclusionary bias.
▷ Recognize issues of equitable access.

■ BEFORE YOU READ THIS CHAPTER

What does it mean to you when something is described as being biased? Are you aware of your own biases? How and why do you think a GenAI platform might be biased?

INTRODUCTION

We tend to say that something is **biased** when it gives advantage to one thing over another in an unfair way. However, bias isn't necessarily a matter of unfairness. For example, a person may prefer the color blue over the color yellow and may, therefore, be biased toward wearing blue clothing rather than yellow. That kind of bias is innocuous. But many other types of bias have impactful social results.

In early 2023, a reporter demonstrated that when ChatGPT was prompted to write an essay in the style of CNN (a liberal-leaning news outlet), it did so without hesitation; but when prompted to write a similar story in the style of the *New York Post* (a conservative-leaning news outlet), it responded that it "cannot generate content that is designed to be inflammatory or biased."[41] This example suggests a worrisome bias in GenAI programs, such that they may favor certain political positions over others.

In the introduction to her important book about bias in technology, *More Than a Glitch* (2023), Meredith Broussard offers an illuminating example.[42] If two kids are arguing over who gets the last cookie in the jar, the parents may decide to break the cookie in half so as to be fair and end the argument. Typically, however, the kids then continue arguing about which half is bigger or which half is better. For a computer, the solution is simple: half equals half. However, that's rarely the case in human social contexts. As Broussard explains, "social fairness and mathematical fairness are different. Computers can only calculate mathematical fairness."[43] This is why computers aren't good at mediating social problems. In fact, as Broussard points out, computers aren't even good at identifying when things are unfair or biased. This is one of the conundrums we face in using GenAI: the AI can't recognize its own biases. Thus, machine–human collaboration requires that we humans be critically alert to the engrained biases in GenAI.

All AI technologies depend on access to data that is human-generated, and they adhere to the functions and rules that human programmers design. AI systems "learn" through each action they engage in, and they train to increase their abilities and their LLMs. As such, they're affected by every instance of use, and can be intentionally or unintentionally trained toward biases as their LLMs expand. For example, an increase in derogatory language on social media regarding a particular politician can affect the linguistic patterns the GenAI identifies in connection with that politician.

According to Alexander Linden, an analyst at the technology research and consulting firm Gartner, "at the moment, there is no way to completely banish bias; however, we have to try our best to reduce it to a minimum."[44] This chapter examines several types of GenAI bias, as well as some methods for addressing or working around those biases.

Provocation

So what if GenAI outputs are biased? What if, in at least some cases, the political biases exhibited by GenAI happen to align with your own beliefs and opinions? If that's the case, is it fair to embrace the biases, or at least to not see them as a problem?

ALGORITHMIC BIAS

Algorithmic bias, sometimes called *machine learning bias*, is any bias that a GenAI exhibits as a result of the ways its algorithms were written. Algorithmic bias occurs when the GenAI privileges specific kinds of information within a data set. This may be the result of a deliberate choice about which data to privilege; or it may simply be the result of some data occurring with disproportionate frequency in a given data set.

One form of algorithmic bias is known as **algorithmic prejudice**. This occurs as a result of bias in the selection of data the GenAI has access to. For example, a GenAI may have access to voter registration data but not to demographic information about those voters. As a result, the GenAI may provide outputs that, in turn, misrepresent the demographic makeup of a given voter population.

Another type of algorithmic bias is **semantic legacy bias**. This occurs when prejudice is engrained in the language used by the GenAI. For example, the data set a GenAI accesses may be dominated by gendered language tropes that are no longer typical. The GenAI might apply male pronouns when referencing doctors, lawyers, or astronauts, simply because those language patterns occur most frequently in the historical data used by the GenAI's LLM.

There are several possible negative outcomes of algorithmic bias:

▷ **Outputs that exhibit representational biases:** If an algorithm's training data is unbalanced or unrepresentative, outcomes may lead to under-representations of some groups.

▷ **Outputs that stereotype:** Because GenAI algorithms look for patterns within a data set, they're likely to perpetuate stereotypes established within those patterns. This means that racist or sexist stereotypes may be reintroduced by a GenAI if they're exhibited in the LLM's dataset. This can be even more of a concern if the dataset relies on a large amount of historical writing.

▷ **Outputs with contextual bias:** GenAI algorithms are typically designed and trained to operate within the perspective of a single generic context. As such, their outputs are often unable to reflect the nuances, complexities, and variabilities of different social groups and settings. Instead of presenting a world of varied cultures and modes of communication, a GenAI's outputs may tend to reflect a homogenized view of people and society.

▷ **Outputs that reflect visual bias:** Visual bias can include the algorithmic privileging of certain skin tones, facial features, body shapes, or beauty standards. AI datasets often include a greater number of associations between some traits than others, and this may be a result of existing social stereotypes or of systemic racism and sexism. For example, there may be a large number of training images in which masculine features are associated with doctors, lawyers, or first responders, leading to those same associations being repeated as outputs. While writing this chapter, I prompted a GenAI platform to produce a photograph-like image of a tattoo artist. All of the four initial images appeared to be Latino/a, presumably because the training data included a disproportionately large number of Latino/a tattoo artists. This kind of visual stereotyping is a result of algorithmic bias.

There are some methods for reducing algorithmic bias. Alexander Linden claims there are technological solutions that can help, such as using diverse datasets; but he also holds that the real key to reducing algorithmic bias is ensuring the demographic diversity of the people working with GenAI.[45] For now, users need to be alert to how algorithmic bias can affect a GenAI's outputs, and should think critically about whether any given output exhibits prejudice.

EXCLUSIONARY BIAS

As we've seen, GenAI outputs can only include data available to the GenAI and its LLM. There are many reasons why some data may be excluded. A great deal of proprietary data is limited in circulation due to copyright and other intellectual property restrictions. For example, a pharmaceutical company's research and development division may limit circulation of information about a new drug.

Algorithms are also unable to access data that hasn't been digitized. Many college and university campus libraries store vast quantities of data that exists only in print and other non-digital formats. This can include books, journals, reports, 8 mm films, photographs, maps, slides, microfiche, and audio tapes. The method of digitization can also affect whether or not an algorithm has access to a given set of data. For example, if a library were to digitize an older public domain print book, it might simply create an image of each page using a scanner or camera. But images of pages can't be read as text unless they undergo further conversion processes, and so they may be excluded from the data accessible to a GenAI. Decisions about when and how to digitize inevitably lead to the exclusion of some data, and this may ultimately lead to bias in a GenAI's output.

Language is another major source of bias. Most AI algorithms are designed to work in only one language—most often English (though more and more GenAI platforms are now being developed in other languages). As a result, the outputs of most GenAI programs favor data conveyed in English and are reflective of Anglophone cultures. Imagine, for example, prompting a GenAI to write about traditional Chinese cooking. If the GenAI's dataset only includes information about Chinese cooking that's been produced in English, it will surely be impoverished, and potentially biased toward cooking techniques and styles more typical of the Anglophone world. The single-language limitations of most GenAI datasets may even lead to what is called "linguistic determinism"—that is, a language and its structures may determine how and what can be thought or communicated. For GenAI, being limited to data from a single language may lead to the exclusion of non-Anglophone ways of understanding and of employing information.

Even within English writing, there are many voices, stories, and bits of information that will never be included in a GenAI's dataset, and thus never reflected in its output. Consider, for example, underground zines of the 1970s and 1980s, or LGBTQ comics from the same time period. Chances are most of these will never be accessible to GenAI data sets because most were distributed as printed materials, never cataloged in any "approved" index, and likely never digitized. Because a GenAI would not find these valuable texts in any LLM, they would not influence the GenAI's output. The same is true for the stories, local knowledge, and artwork of Indigenous Americans, African Americans, Asian Americans, and the many other diverse groups whose voices outside the mainstream are far less frequently preserved or digitized.

In these ways, the data that is excluded from LLM data sets can lead to substantial and even harmful biases. Users should be aware of such biases when using GenAI-produced content.

EQUITABLE ACCESS

There are other aspects of GenAI that can be exclusionary, such as inequality of access. **Equitable access** to GenAI is the idea that everyone should be equally able to utilize the technologies and resources needed for human–GenAI collaboration. These include access to broadband internet, GenAI platforms, and devices capable of running those platforms.

You've probably said many times, "this internet connection sucks," as you stare at a slow-loading app. We've grown so accustomed to having ubiquitous high-speed internet that we get frustrated when we don't have it. We rely on internet access for education, healthcare, employment, and even housing, and some are even calling for the United Nations to declare internet access a basic human right. However, the reality is that not everyone has internet access, even in the US. There are large areas in the American southwest where people simply don't have access to broadband internet due to geographic limitations.[46] The Appalachian Regional Commission reports that only 89.5 per cent of Appalachian residents have computer access, 80.9 per cent have smart phone access, and 82.8 per cent have access to broadband.[47]

In addition to geographic inequity, some people simply can't afford the internet or appropriate computing devices such as cellphones or laptops. The commercialization of GenAI is financially exclusionary too: as more companies develop GenAI applications that operate on subscription models, only those who can afford them will benefit.

In any given class, one student may be able to afford high-speed internet, a cutting-edge mobile device, and subscriptions to the highest-end GenAI platforms available; another may have no internet access at home whatsoever, and may rely on only a dated cellphone as a computing device. This inequity gives wealthier students advantages that are further exacerbated by the emergence of paid GenAI programs. This is why equitable access must be paramount when considering the use of GenAI in education.

END OF CHAPTER MATERIALS

So What?

1. There is some risk in neglecting to expect or account for bias when using GenAI programs. So what? Is this any different from the risks we would face in working with other human authors?

2. GenAI cannot itself identify bias in either the data it accesses or in its outputs. So what? What role must GenAI users play in addressing bias?

Conceptual AI

1. One of the biases of many GenAI LLMs is that the datasets from which they draw tend to exclude some perspectives and voices while privileging others. How might you alleviate the effects of these kinds of biases when working with GenAI?

2. Do you think it will ever be possible to devise GenAI tools that are inherently resistant to biases, or that eliminate bias altogether? Why or why not?

Applied AI

1. Prompt a GenAI program to write an answer in response to this question: "What are the biggest hurdles to overcome in [your career path]?" Then analyze the response for elements that may be biased.

2. Using a GenAI platform that creates images, enter a prompt for an image of a person in a particular profession without providing details about age, gender, or race. What's the first image the GenAI returns? Now, try a revised prompt containing specific details about age, gender, and race. What's the first image the GenAI returns for the revised prompt? Do the two images differ substantially in any ways other than age, gender, or race?

3. What are some strategies you might employ for testing a GenAI's algorithms and its LLM for bias? Develop an assessment strategy for checking the biases of a GenAI platform that you can deploy before making use of that program's outputs.

For Discussion

1. After reading this chapter, has your thinking about GenAI changed? Has the information in this chapter altered how you think about GenAI or how you might use GenAI in the future? Discuss the ways in which understanding GenAI biases will impact your use of the technology.

2. What do you see as some of the biggest risks regarding GenAI bias? Consider the many different contexts in which writing takes place: academic, professional, civic, and personal. Do the risks vary by context? How can you be alert to and account for these risks?

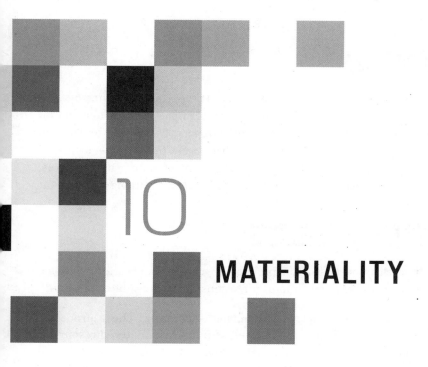

MATERIALITY

10

■ LEARNING OBJECTIVES ■■■■■■■■■■■■■■■■■■■■

▷ Describe the role of cradle-to-grave thinking in relation to GenAI technologies.

▷ Understand the unique environmental and social impact of GenAI training processes.

▷ Recognize the economic, social, and environmental consequences of using modern electronics.

■ BEFORE YOU READ THIS CHAPTER ■■■■■■■■■■■■■

Consider the various devices involved in GenAI. On the user end, these include smart phones, laptops, tablets, and desktop computers. For the GenAI manufacturers and providers, they include countless servers, powerful specialized processors, and all of the electronics used for research, development, and operations. What are those devices made from? What happens when they break, or when they're replaced with newer versions? If we extend this picture further, we find that a huge amount of additional resources—including heavy equipment and fuel—is also required for all of the processes involved in GenAI: manufacturing, distribution, and disposal. With all of this taken into account, what are the material impacts of GenAI?

INTRODUCTION

Materiality encompasses not just the physical properties of a technology, but also its economic, social, and environmental impacts. As the demand for GenAI increases, so too does its material impact. To properly understand this impact, we must examine GenAI's full life cycle, from "cradle" to "grave." This chapter offers a very brief overview of some of these material factors, so that you can better understand the hidden costs of working with GenAI.

POINTS OF MATERIAL IMPACT

The lifecycle impacts of digital products are complex and varied. However, some steps are especially important to consider in the context of GenAI:

1. **Research, development, design, and engineering:** These processes involve significant labor as well as numerous material resources, including the computers that engineers use for their work and all of the surrounding infrastructure.

    In the case of GenAI, it's important to factor in the impacts of the training process whereby an LLM is produced and refined. Sasha Luccioni, a researcher at the machine learning company HuggingFace, recently attempted to calculate these impacts:

    > Depending on the energy source used for training and its carbon intensity, training a 2022-era LLM emits at least 25 metric tons of carbon equivalents if you use renewable energy.... If you use carbon-intensive energy sources like coal and natural gas, which was the case for GPT-3, this number quickly goes up to 500 metric tons of carbon emissions, roughly equivalent to over a million miles driven by an average gasoline-powered car.[48]

    The process of training LLMs also involves substantial human labor. Luccioni succinctly describes this process and why it may concern us:

    > Essentially, once a model has been trained on large quantities of unlabeled data (from the web, books, etc.), humans are then asked to interact with the model, coming up with

prompts (e.g., "Write me a recipe for chocolate cake") and provide their own answers or evaluate answers provided by the model. This data is used to continue training the model, which is then again tested by humans, *ad nauseam*, until the model is deemed good enough to be released into the world.... But that success has a dirty secret behind it: To keep the costs of AI low, the people providing this "human feedback" are underpaid, overexploited workers. In January [2023], *Time* wrote a report about Kenyan laborers paid less than $2 an hour to examine thousands of messages for OpenAI.[49] This kind of work can have long-lasting psychological impacts, as we've seen in content-moderation workers.[50]

2. **Component sourcing and manufacturing:** This can involve the production of processors, memory chips, displays, batteries, camera modules, sensors, connectors, and other electronic parts. The electronics used to provide and operate GenAI require significant amounts of resource extraction, leading to both social and environmental harms.

3. **Disposal:** The disposal of used and broken electronics can be surprisingly dangerous and environmentally impactful. Though the software involved in GenAI doesn't itself require hazardous disposal, the creation and use of GenAI requires a substantial number of electronic products that must eventually be disposed of.

The remaining sections of this chapter discuss the second and third of these factors.

THE CRADLE: EXTRACTION

We know—even if we don't often think about it—that our devices are manufactured from various chemicals and minerals. Among these are tin (which is extracted primarily from cassiterite), tungsten (extracted from wolframite), and tantalum (extracted from coltan). Tin is a primary component in the soldering of computer circuit boards, and most of the cassiterite needed for tin extraction is mined in Bolivia, China, Indonesia, Malaysia, Myanmar, Nigeria, and Thailand. Wolframite is extracted in Australia, England, Germany, Myanmar, Portugal, Spain and the Malay

Peninsula. And approximately 80 per cent of the world's coltan is mined in the Democratic Republic of Congo.

Given the transnational origins of these minerals, it's important to ask questions about the impacts of their extraction and use. With regard to resource extraction, there are three primary categories of ethical concern: 1. conflict over resources in the regions where they're extracted, 2. forced labor and the use of slavery to extract resources, and 3. the environmental impacts of the extraction process.

Conflict resources are those that are produced from within a conflict zone. The sale of these resources helps fund the war efforts of those who control them. Many of the minerals used in electronic manufacturing function as conflict resources in the Democratic Republic of Congo. The sale of these resources has funded the Congolese National Army, several rebel military groups, the Democratic Forces for the Liberation of Rwanda, and the National Congress for the Defense of the People, a proxy Rwandan militia group. In both the first and second Congo Wars (1996–97 and 1998–2003), Rwanda, Uganda, and Burundi relied on the profits from conflict resources to fund war efforts. It's estimated that since 1996 more than 6 million people have died in the civil wars in the DRC region, which is heavily funded by resource extraction, and in turn partly fueled by our demanded for new electronic devices.[51]

Provocation

How should you negotiate between (a) the social benefits of digital literacy and communication, (b) your personal desire for electronics, and (c) ethical concerns about the social impacts and possible harms caused by the extraction of resources used to produce electronics?

In addition to thinking about the political and international conflicts fueled by resource extraction, we must also consider the ecological ramifications of mineral harvest. Mining has extensive ecological and environmental effects. Even regulated mines in places we don't associate with conflict issues can still create environmentally harmful results; for example:

▷ The Britannia Mine: a former copper mine near Vancouver, British Columbia, leaked chemicals into local waters, contaminating those waters for years even after the mine closed. The contaminated waters flowed into Howe Sound, making the area near the mining facility the most polluted part of the 27-mile Sound.

▷ The Tar Creek Mine: located in Picher, Oklahoma, produced lead, zinc, cadmium, and arsenic. These chemicals leached from the mine into local ground water, making it one of the most toxic areas in the US. The site is now an Environmental Protection Agency Superfund site.

THE GRAVE: DISPOSAL AND E-WASTE

According to the World Economic Forum (WEF), electronic waste or **e-waste**—which consists primarily of discarded electronic devices—is the fastest growing waste stream in the world.[52] The rapid development of new technologies such as GenAI fuels increases in e-waste as it increases demand for new electronics, both on the user end and on the side of producers and distributors. China, followed closely by the US, produces the most e-waste.[53] E-waste is responsible for 70 per cent of the overall toxic waste disposed of each year. We only recycle about 12.5 per cent of our e-waste, and roughly 85 per cent of it is transported to landfills—often in China, Southeast Asia, or Africa—or incinerated, releasing toxic chemicals into the groundwater or into the atmosphere.[54]

E-waste raises a number of ethical challenges:

▷ **Recycling challenges:** Because of the toxicity of many of the components used to make digital devices, recycling e-waste is difficult. Most electronic components aren't biodegradable. The processes involved in manually separating and extracting minerals from discarded electronics can place workers at risk of contact with toxic chemicals, and can involve the release of toxic chemicals into the air, land, or water.

▷ **Resource depletion:** Inefficient recycling also contributes to ongoing depletion of the materials needed to make digital devices.

▷ **Global trade and dumping:** The US exports a significant portion of its e-waste to developing countries, which often have less stringent regulations for disposal and recycling. E-waste disposal and recycling provide economic benefits to these regions, but also exacerbate environmental pollution and health hazards for workers involved in these processes. And in many cases, exportation leads to materials being buried or incinerated in ways that take advantage of the recipient country's laxer regulations.

The extent of our e-waste can in part be addressed through policies and public awareness campaigns. These can include extended producer responsibility programs, promotional campaigns for responsible recycling practices, policies requiring that devices be repairable and upgradable, and awareness campaigns regarding the environmental and social impacts of e-waste. While the emergence and evolution of GenAI is certainly a contributing factor to the e-waste problem, it may also be worth consulting GenAI in search of potential solutions (see the exercises below for ideas).

END OF CHAPTER MATERIALS

So What?

1. We use all sorts of products and services that have substantial environmental impacts. So what? What's the problem with using even more of them, including GenAI?

2. Most often, we don't see exactly what happens to our devices once we've disposed of them. So what difference does it make to us as individuals? Should we care about the impacts of our own individual contributions to e-waste if they're likely to have little bearing on the big picture?

Conceptual AI

1. The material impacts of Generative AI's creation and use are substantial, from its impacts on e-waste to its role in conflict resources and

human rights violations. However, understanding and awareness don't necessarily lead to action. After reading this chapter, are you likely to take a different approach to your own interactions with GenAI?

2. When you use a digital device such as a smart phone or a laptop, how much time do you spend considering the material aspects of its construction and disposal? Do the intricacies of what it took to make the device matter to you? Why or why not?

3. Educational institutions produce a tremendous amount of e-waste. Locate your college or university's policy toward e-waste disposal (if it has one). Does your school have a contract with an organization that disposes of e-waste? If it does, investigate that organization. Where does it take the waste? Has it been independently audited or reviewed? Create an infographic or other visual to show the path your institution's e-waste takes.

Applied AI

1. Use a GenAI platform to conduct research on one aspect of materiality discussed in this chapter. Revise and refine your prompts to the GenAI until you have a core set of resulting information that could be used to inform others. Next, convert that information into some form of distributable output, such as a short animation, an infographic, a social media post, or a web-based interactive page.

2. Using a GenAI platform, explore the possibilities for a new approach to any one of the problems examined in this chapter. For example, work with the GenAI to develop one or more innovative ideas for increasing the proportion of recycled electronics.

3. Much more could be said about material impacts and the technical uses of each of the component resources involved in GenAI production and operation. Research one of these resources, such as tin, tungsten, or tantalum. Explain the ways that GenAI relies on that material. Trace in greater detail the ways in which that resource is extracted or manufactured. Is it a conflict resource? Is it tied to harmful environmental practices? What typically happens to it at end of lifecycle—is it often recycled?

For Discussion

1. Discuss the importance or irrelevance of the issues addressed in this chapter. Why aren't the material impacts of electronics more often discussed? Should we take them into account at all when evaluating our practices and policies toward GenAI if we aren't already doing the same for other electronic goods and services?

2. I recently asked a friend who'd bought a new smart phone what she'd done with her old one. "I threw it out," she told me. When I pointed out that improper disposal could have an environmental impact, her response was one of ambivalence: "Yeah, so what? It's trash." Her response is not unusual; most people I speak with either don't care about or don't want to acknowledge the material impacts of the devices they use. Why do you suppose this apathy is so prevalent? Is there something about the size, appearance, and marketing of electronics that makes us less likely to consider their material impacts than we might with, say, inefficient motor vehicles or food waste?

NOTES

1   Katharina Buchholz and Felix Richter, "Infographic: ChatGPT Sprints to One Million Users," *Statista*, 24 Jan. 2023.

2   UBS, "How Long It Took Top Apps to Hit 100M Monthly Users," *Yahoo! News*, https://ca.news.yahoo.com/chatgpt-on-track-to-surpass-100-million-users-faster-than-tiktok-or-instagram-ubs-214423357.html. Accessed Aug. 4, 2023.

3   Lyss Welding, "Half of College Students Say Using AI on Schoolwork Is Cheating or Plagiarism," *Best Colleges*, 27 Mar. 2023, https://www.bestcolleges.com/research/college-students-ai-tools-survey.

4   Ken Schwencke, "Earthquake: 4.7 Quake Strikes Near Lone Pine," *Los Angeles Times*, 23 Dec. 2013, https://www.latimes.com/local/lanow/earthquake-47-quake-strikes-near-lone-pine-california-s6emrv-story.html.

5   Welding.

6   Kanta Dihal, "Enslaved Minds: Artificial Intelligence, Slavery, and Revolt," in Stephen Cave, et al., *AI Narratives: A History of Imaginative Thinking about Intelligent Machines*. Oxford University Press, 2020, pp. 196–97.

7   A.M. Turing, "Computing Machinery and Intelligence," *Mind*, vol. 59, 1950, pp. 433–60.

8   "Write an academic biography of Sidney I. Dobrin" prompt. *ChatGPT* 3.0, 15 Mar. version, OpenAI, 28 Apr. 2023, chat.openai.com/chat.

9   "Hands playing on a piano" prompt. *Dall-E* 2, OpenAI, 15 Jul. 2023, labs.openai.com.

10 "Beneficial AI 2017," *Future of Life Institute*, 12 Jan. 2017, https://futureoflife.org/event/bai-2017/.

11 "Pause Giant AI Experiments: An Open Letter," *Future of Life Institute*, 22 Mar. 2023, https://futureoflife.org/open-letter/pause-giant-ai-experiments/.

12 Owen Kichizo Terry, "I'm a Student. You Have No Idea How Much We're Using ChatGPT," *The Chronicle of Higher Education*, 12 May 2023, https://www.chronicle.com/article/im-a-student-you-have-no-idea-how-much-were-using-chatgpt.

13 "How Do I Cite Generative AI in MLA Style?," *MLA Style Center*, 17 Mar. 2023, https://style.mla.org/citing-generative-ai/.

14 "How Do I Cite Generative AI in MLA Style?"

15 "How Do I Cite Generative AI in MLA Style?"

16 Timothy McAdoo, "How to Cite ChatGPT," *APA Style Blog*, 7 Apr. 2023, https://apastyle.apa.org/blog/how-to-cite-chatgpt.

17 McAdoo.

18 "IEEE Referencing: Unpublished Material," *Victoria University Library Guides*, https://libraryguides.vu.edu.au/ieeereferencing/personalcommunication. Accessed Aug. 4, 2023.

19   "Revise this paragraph into an informal style" prompt. *ChatGPT* 4.0, 24 May version, OpenAI, 9 Jul. 2023, chat.openai.com/chat.

20   "Revise the paragraph again, making it less wordy and more professional yet still informal" prompt. *ChatGPT* 4.0, 24 May version, OpenAI, 9 Jul. 2023, chat.openai.com/chat.

21   "Replace only the verbs in this passage (including 'is'), using more exciting verbs" prompt. *ChatGPT* 4.0, 24 May version, OpenAI, 9 Jul. 2023, chat.openai.com/chat.

22   "Expert Opinion: Episode 30 with Professor Cath Ellis & Stephen Matchett," *YouTube*, uploaded by Twig Marketing, 16 Mar. 2023, https://www.youtube.com/watch?v=FpevM_kdhjg.

23   "Open Competition 2023," *Sony*, 3 Mar. 2023, https://www.sony-asia.com/pressrelease?prName=open-competition-2023.

24   Boris Eldagsen, "Sony World Photography Awards 2023," 14 Mar. 2023, https://www.eldagsen.com/sony-world-photography-awards-2023/.

25   Hany Farid of the UC Berkeley School of Information has published numerous examples of manipulated photographs throughout history.

26   "A photographic quality image of a shark wearing a space helmet" prompt. *Dall-E* 2, OpenAI, 15 Jul. 2023, labs.openai.com.

27   "A golden retriever jumping to catch a ball; the fur of the dog resembles an almond dipped in honey" prompt. *Dall-E* 2, OpenAI, 15 Jul. 2023, labs.openai.com.

28   "The open ocean early in the morning just as the sun rises on the horizon. There are a few rain clouds in the background. Two gulls fly by. The air is clear with no haze" prompt. *Dall-E* 2, OpenAI, 15 Jul. 2023, labs.openai.com.

29   "A dilapidated factory, conveying a nostalgic sensation" and "A dilapidated factory, conveying a feeling of palpable tension" prompts. *Dall-E* 2, OpenAI, 15 Jul. 2023, labs.openai.com.

30   "A close-up photograph of an arm-wrestling contest" prompt. *Dall-E* 2, OpenAI, 15 Jul. 2023, labs.openai.com.

31   "Coca-Cola Masterpiece," *YouTube*, uploaded by Coca-Cola, 6 Mar. 2023, https://www.youtube.com/watch?v=VGa1imApfdg.

32   Allison Parshall, "How This AI Image Won a Major Photography Competition," *Scientific American*, 21 Apr. 2023, https://www.scientificamerican.com/article/how-my-ai-image-won-a-major-photography-competition/.

33   *The Future of Jobs Report 2023*, World Economic Forum, 30 Apr. 2023, p. 30.

34   *The Future of Jobs Report 2023*, p. 6.

35   *The Future of Jobs Report 2023*, p. 25.

36   Sandra Stotsky, "Civic Writing in Education for Democratic Citizenship," *ERIC Digest*, July 1999, p. 2, https://eric.ed.gov/?id=ED431706.

37   Stotsky, pp. 2–3.

38   *Sizing the Prize: What's the Real Value of AI for Your Business and How Can You Capitalise?* PWC, 2017, https://www.pwc.com/gx/en/issues/data-and-analytics/publications/artificial-intelligence-study.html.

39 *The Future of Jobs Report 2023*, p. 30.

40 *The Future of Jobs Report 2023*, p. 46.

41 Alex Mitchell, "Great—Now 'Liberal' ChatGPT Is Censoring *The Post*'s Hunter Biden Coverage, Too," *New York Post*, 14 Feb. 2023, https://nypost.com/2023/02/14/chatgpt-censors-new-york-post-coverage-of-hunter-biden/.

42 Meredith Broussard, *More Than a Glitch: Confronting Race, Gender, and Ability Bias in Tech*. MIT Press, 2023, pp. 1–2.

43 Broussard, p. 2.

44 "6 AI Myths Debunked," *Gartner*, 5 Nov. 2019, https://www.gartner.com/smarterwithgartner/5-ai-myths-debunked.

45 "6 AI Myths Debunked."

46 "FCC National Broadband Map," *Federal Communications Commission*, https://broadbandmap.fcc.gov/home. Accessed Aug. 4, 2023.

47 "Computer and Broadband Access in Appalachia," *Appalachian Regional Commission*, https://www.arc.gov/about-the-appalachian-region/the-chart-book/computer-and-broadband-access-in-appalachia/. Accessed Aug. 4, 2023.

48 Sasha Luccioni, "The Mounting Human and Environmental Costs of Generative AI," *Ars Technica*, 12 Apr. 2023, https://arstechnica.com/gadgets/2023/04/generative-ai-is-cool-but-lets-not-forget-its-human-and-environmental-costs/.

49 Billy Perrigo, "Exclusive: OpenAI Used Kenyan Workers on Less Than $2 Per Hour to Make ChatGPT Less Toxic," *Time*, 18 Jan. 2023, https://time.com/6247678/openai-chatgpt-kenya-workers/.

50 Luccioni.

51 Center for Preventive Action, "Conflict in the Democratic Republic of Congo," *Global Conflict Tracker*, https://www.cfr.org/global-conflict-tracker/conflict/violence-democratic-republic-congo. Accessed Aug. 4, 2023.

52 Jon Smieja, "The Enormous Opportunity of E-Waste Recycling," *World Economic Forum*, 24 Mar. 2023, https://www.weforum.org/agenda/2023/03/the-enormous-opportunity-of-e-waste-recycling/.

53 "Leading Countries Based on Generation of Electronic Waste Worldwide in 2019," *Statista*, 2023, https://www.statista.com/statistics/499952/ewaste-generation-worldwide-by-major-country/.

54 "Electronic Waste Facts," *The World Counts*, https://www.theworldcounts.com/stories/electronic-waste-facts. Accessed Aug. 4, 2023.

IMAGE CREDITS

Page 18   ENIAC (Electronic Numerical Integrator and Computer) in Philadelphia, Pennsylvania, c. 1947–55, https://commons.wikimedia.org/wiki/File:Eniac.jpg.

Page 19   Angler fish: Olga1969, CC BY 4.0, https://commons.wikimedia.org/wiki/File:Angler_fish.jpg; Trout: Eric Engbretson, US Fish and Wildlife Service, https://commons.wikimedia.org/wiki/File:Salmo_trutta.jpg. Blobfish: https://commons.wikimedia.org/wiki/File:Psychrolutes_phrictus.jpg;

Page 38   Copyright © Sidney Harris, ScienceCartoonsPlus.com.

Page 69   DOONESBURY © 2023 G.B. Trudeau. Reprinted with permission of ANDREWS MCMEEL SYNDICATION. All rights reserved.

Page 72   Boris Eldagsen, *PSEUDOMNESIA: The Electrician,* 2023. Reprinted with permission.

Page 75   Sean Linehan, "Salmon Fishing with Large Loop Nets by Native Americans," NOAA Historic Fisheries Collection, https://commons.wikimedia.org/wiki/File:Salmon_fishing_with_large_loop_nets_by_Native_Americans.jpg.

INDEX

academic integrity, 12, 31, 32–33, 43–45; and citation, 52; and plagiarism, 34, 35, 36, 37; and transparency and documentation, 39; *see also* citation styles

Adobe's "Generative Fill," 75

AI algorithms, 21

"AI and Machine Learning Specialist," 86, 96, 97

AI Literacy, 96

AI promptives, 69; *see also* prompts

algorithmic bias (or machine learning bias), 105–07

AnyWord, 85

Applied AI, 8, 13–14, 29–30, 62, 70, 81, 100–01, 110, 117; *see also* Conceptual AI

arrangement, 53–54

Artificial Intelligence (AI), first coined, 18; and identifying fish in pictures, 20, 22; origins of, 16–20; *see also* neural network

Asilomar Principles, 29

Associated Press, The, 4

Aviva, 85

basic mathematics and computation, 99

Beneficial AI conference (2017), 29

Best Colleges, 3, 4, 12

biases, 51, 67, 103, 104–05, 108, 109, 110; algorithmic bias, 105–07; contextual bias, 106; exclusionary bias, 107–08; machine learning bias, 105–07; political biases, 105, 109; representational biases, 106; semantic legacy bias, 105; visual bias, 106

big data, 96, 98

Bloomberg News, 4

Boomy, 85

Bronson, Rachel, 29

Broussard, Meredith, *More Than a Glitch* (2023), 104

Čapek, Karel, *R.U.R.* (*Rossum's Universal Robots*), 17

careers, GenAI-related, 4, 28, 70, 95, 98, 99; *see also* jobs

chatbots, ix, 4, 10, 13, 23, 50

Chat Generative Pre-trained Transformer (ChatGPT), 13, 15, 23, 30, 42, 44, 48, 50, 52, 58, 70, 76, 85; citing, 40–42; introduction and impact of, ix, 2–3, 7, 17; writes a biography, 25–27; writes an essay, 104; *see also* Terry

Cicero, *De Inventione*, 48–49

citation, 36, 39; benefits of, 52

citation styles: APA (American Psychological Association), 36, 40–41; Chicago, 36; IEEE (Institute of Electrical and Electronics Engineers), 36, 41–42; MLA (Modern Language Association), 36, 39–40; Turabian, 36

class assignments and GenAI, 53

CodeSquire, 85

CodeWP, 85

Codex, 85

collaborative writing, 9, 90

communication skills, 99

concealment, 80

From the Publisher

A name never says it all, but the word "Broadview" expresses a good deal
of the philosophy behind our company. We are open to a broad range of
academic approaches and political viewpoints. We pay attention to the
broad impact book publishing and book printing has in the wider world;
for some years now we have used 100% recycled paper for most titles.
Our publishing program is internationally oriented and broad-ranging.
Our individual titles often appeal to a broad readership too; many are
of interest as much to general readers as to academics and students.

Founded in 1985, Broadview remains a fully independent
company owned by its shareholders—not an imprint
or subsidiary of a larger multinational.

To order our books or obtain up-to-date information, please visit
broadviewpress.com.

broadview press
www.broadviewpress.com

MIX
Paper | Supporting
responsible forestry
FSC® C013916
FSC
www.fsc.org

The interior of this book is printed on 100% recycled paper.